Benches to make at home

If you cannot afford a ready-made bench, you can make your own bench fairly cheaply. Here are two basic designs.

The sturdy timber-framed bench, which is 830 mm. (32¾ in.) high and has a 1500 × 600 mm. (5 × 2 ft) top, can be made for less than half the cost of a ready-made bench of the same size.

Bolt the front and back rails to the inner faces of the legs so that their top edges are about 250 mm. (10 in.) above the floor.

Screw a side panel firmly to the outer edges of each pair of legs, flush with the tops and overlapping the back legs by

18 mm. (¾ in.). It is important that these side panels are truly square.

Bolt a side rail to the inner edge of each pair of legs, flush with the tops and outer faces of the legs.

Screw the back panel to the back rail and back legs.

Cut the shelf to fit inside the frame and around the back legs, finishing flush with the front face of the front rail. Screw it to the front and back rails.

Make the top by gluing and screwing together two 1500 × 600 mm. sheets of 18 mm. block-board. Drill holes for three

150 mm. (6 in.) coach bolts at each end of the top for fixing it to the side rails. Counterbore the holes so that the bolt heads are set below the surface.

Position the top on the underframe to overlap the back panel by about 25 mm. (1 in.). Bolt the top firmly to the side rails.

Cover the top with a 1500 × 600 mm. sheet of 6 mm. oil-tempered hardboard, using contact adhesive.

If you are going to fit a woodworker's vice to the bench, lip the front edge of the top with a strip of 42 × 22 mm. (1¾ × ⅞ in.) hardwood, for a better working edge.

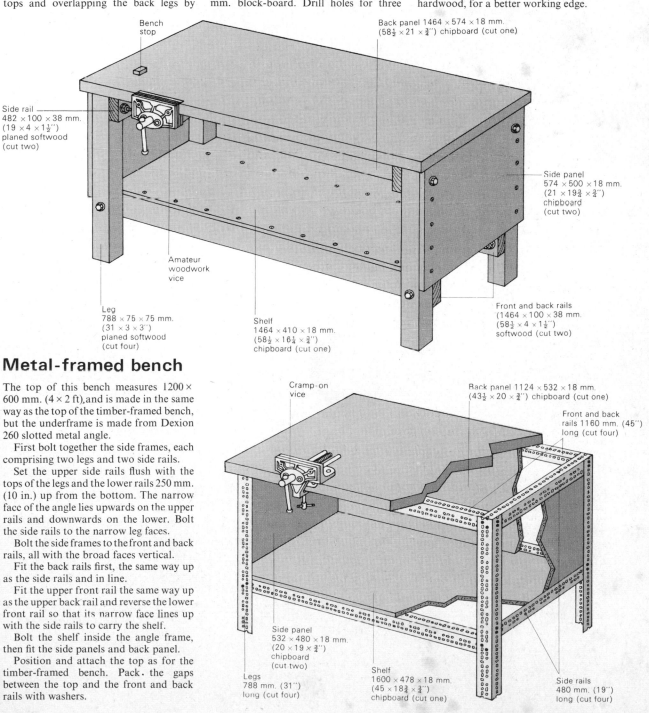

Bench stop

Side rail
482 × 100 × 38 mm.
(19 × 4 × 1½″)
planed softwood
(cut two)

Back panel 1464 × 574 × 18 mm.
(58½ × 21 × ¾″) chipboard (cut one)

Side panel
574 × 500 × 18 mm.
(21 × 19¾ × ¾″)
chipboard
(cut two)

Amateur woodwork vice

Leg
788 × 75 × 75 mm.
(31 × 3 × 3″)
planed softwood
(cut four)

Shelf
1464 × 410 × 18 mm.
(58½ × 16¼ × ¾″)
chipboard (cut one)

Front and back rails
(1464 × 100 × 38 mm.
(58½ × 4 × 1½″)
softwood (cut two)

Metal-framed bench

The top of this bench measures 1200 × 600 mm. (4 × 2 ft), and is made in the same way as the top of the timber-framed bench, but the underframe is made from Dexion 260 slotted metal angle.

First bolt together the side frames, each comprising two legs and two side rails.

Set the upper side rails flush with the tops of the legs and the lower rails 250 mm. (10 in.) up from the bottom. The narrow face of the angle lies upwards on the upper rails and downwards on the lower. Bolt the side rails to the narrow leg faces.

Bolt the side frames to the front and back rails, all with the broad faces vertical.

Fit the back rails first, the same way up as the side rails and in line.

Fit the upper front rail the same way up as the upper back rail and reverse the lower front rail so that its narrow face lines up with the side rails to carry the shelf.

Bolt the shelf inside the angle frame, then fit the side panels and back panel.

Position and attach the top as for the timber-framed bench. Pack the gaps between the top and the front and back rails with washers.

Cramp-on vice

Back panel 1124 × 532 × 18 mm.
(43½ × 20 × ¾″) chipboard (cut one)

Front and back rails 1160 mm. (45″) long (cut four)

Side panel
532 × 480 × 18 mm.
(20 × 19 × ¾″)
chipboard
(cut two)

Legs
788 mm. (31″)
long (cut four)

Shelf
1600 × 478 × 18 mm.
(45 × 18¾ × ¾″)
chipboard (cut one)

Side rails
480 mm. (19″)
long (cut four)

Tools/3

Choosing a vice

The most important bench accessory is a woodworking vice—the bigger the better, as the principal requirement of a vice is that it grips wood over the largest possible area.

The big steel woodworker's vices built into ready-made benches (see p. 2) can be bought with or without a quick-release mechanism. This is operated by a lever that disengages the main screw from the nut so that the front jaw can be slid rapidly in either direction. The main screw has to be used only for final tightening of the jaws.

One type of woodworker's vice with quick-release mechanism is also fitted with an adjustable front dog, so that it can be used to cramp a wide piece of timber flat on the bench, holding it against a stop at the back of the bench. A vice like this will compensate to some extent for the absence of an end-screw vice.

Less expensive than a woodworker's vice is the 150 mm. (6 in.) Amateur woodwork vice. This is bolted to the underside of a bench top. Cut away the front edge of the bench so that the rear jaw of the vice, when fitted with a protective wooden plate, falls flush with the bench edge.

If you do not have room for a permanent bench, you can make a good temporary substitute by cramping a vice on to a strong kitchen table, directly above a leg.

The Stanley 5702 aluminium vice has an offset cramp which allows it to be fixed to the front or side of the work surface.

Surface-mounted vices are generally less effective than flush-mounted types because of their narrower and shallower jaws. Their usefulness is also more limited because they hold the work above the level of the bench top.

However, in many cases when the amount of work is small, or only limited space is available, the high cost of a big vice is not justified.

A vice is only for gripping. Never tighten it so that it crushes the work.

Hold objects that are narrower than the jaws in the centre of the vice whenever possible. If you have to grip an object at the outside of the jaws, use a piece of wood of identical thickness at the other side to balance the grip. This prevents strain and possible distortion of the vice.

No woodworking vice is designed to withstand heavy hammering.

A very useful accessory for use with a flush-mounted vice is a bench 'leg'. This is used for supporting long lengths of timber.

A bench stop is needed to hold timber steady while it is being planed on the bench top. There are two retractable types that can be lowered to provide an unobstructed flat surface.

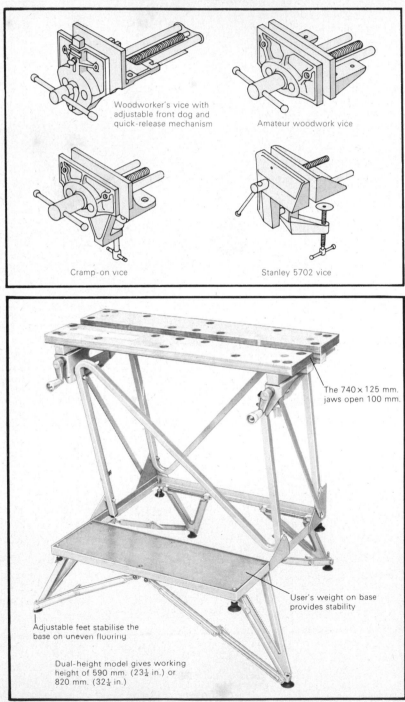

Woodworker's vice with adjustable front dog and quick-release mechanism

Amateur woodwork vice

Cramp-on vice

Stanley 5702 vice

The 740 × 125 mm. jaws open 100 mm.

User's weight on base provides stability

Adjustable feet stabilise the base on uneven flooring

Dual-height model gives working height of 590 mm. (23¼ in.) or 820 mm. (32¼ in.)

The Workmate folds for storage and can be hung on special wall brackets.

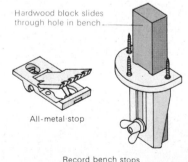

Hardwood block slides through hole in bench

All-metal stop

Record bench stops

The all-metal stop is let into the bench top, the other is fixed to the underside and has a hardwood block that slides through a hole cut in the top.

When there is not room for a permanent workbench and a big vice, the folding Black and Decker Workmate offers a combination of vice, bench and sawhorse.

The 740mm. (29 in.) long jaws operate in taper to grip irregular-shaped objects or in parallel to hold big boards. The normal opening is up to 100 mm. (4 in.), but this can be extended to 250 mm. (10 in.) using vice pegs. Power tools and vices can be mounted on the jaws, which can also be used as a seat. There are two models, single and dual height.

READER'S DIGEST BASIC GUIDE

WORKING IN WOOD

Contents

Tools 2
BENCHES, SAWS, PLANES, CHISELS

Woods 21
TYPES OF WOOD, BUYING

Measuring 30
SQUARES, RULES, PLUMB-BOBS

Joints 36
T-JOINTS, L-JOINTS

Fixing 46
HAMMERS, SCREWDRIVERS, DRILLS

Finishing 58
SANDING, POLISHING

THE TEXT AND ILLUSTRATIONS IN THIS BOOK ARE TAKEN
FROM THE READER'S DIGEST COMPLETE DO-IT-YOURSELF MANUAL
PUBLISHED BY THE READER'S DIGEST ASSOCIATION LIMITED
LONDON   NEW YORK   CAPE TOWN   MONTREAL   SYDNEY

Tools/1

Equipment for an ideal work-area

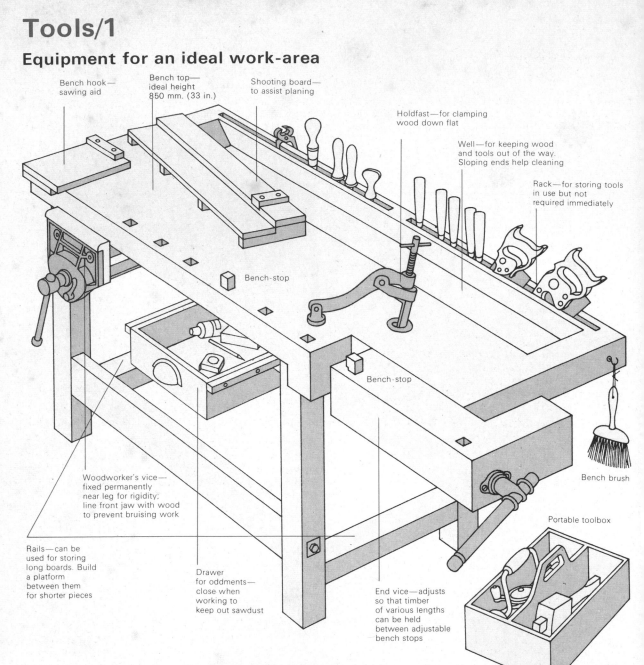

Bench hook—
sawing aid

Bench top—
ideal height
850 mm. (33 in.)

Shooting board—
to assist planing

Holdfast—for clamping
wood down flat

Well—for keeping wood
and tools out of the way.
Sloping ends help cleaning

Rack—for storing tools
in use but not
required immediately

Bench-stop

Bench-stop

Bench brush

Woodworker's vice—
fixed permanently
near leg for rigidity;
line front jaw with wood
to prevent bruising work

Rails—can be
used for storing
long boards. Build
a platform
between them
for shorter pieces

Drawer
for oddments—
close when
working to
keep out sawdust

End vice—adjusts
so that timber
of various lengths
can be held
between adjustable
bench stops

Portable toolbox

Ready-made joiner's bench is fitted with woodworker's vice and end vice.

The first piece of equipment you need for using hand tools is a rigid, flat work surface to support timber while it is sawn, planed, fitted and polished.

The ideal set-up is provided by the traditional joiner's bench, made of beech, which stands up to heavy use yet is soft enough not to bruise work or damage tools that are placed on it.

The bench top must be kept flat and in good condition, so always use a bench hook or spare piece of wood between the work and the bench when hammering, drilling, chiselling or sawing. Always do any hammering directly above the legs—the most solid areas of the bench.

Solid bench tops occasionally need truing-up. Plane diagonally in each direction with your longest plane and complete the job by planing along the grain.

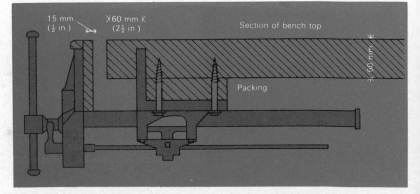

15 mm.
(½ in.)

60 mm.
(2½ in.)

Section of bench top

Packing

50 mm. (2 in.)

Fitting a woodworker's vice. Cut a groove under the bench top to take the rear jaw of the vice and screw the vice to the bench top through a packing piece.

Fitted this way, a 230 mm. (9 in.) vice still has an effective opening of about 250 mm. (10 in.) and the bench edge offers a flat area for holding long work.

Which tools to buy first

A basic tool kit can be supplemented logically so that each additional tool adds to the range of work that can be undertaken. When you have the basic tools listed here, a more specialised collection can be made according to individual needs.

1. 450 gm. (16 oz.) claw hammer; pin punch, 2·5 mm. ($\frac{3}{32}$ in.) point. For simple jointing, general nailing work and setting nails below the surface before painting.
2. 560 mm. (22 in.) ten-point panel saw. For general cutting with or across the grain on softwood up to 63 mm (2½ in.) thick (see 9, Tenon saw).
3. Saw file; saw set. For saw maintenance, unless you prefer to send your saw away to be doctored.
4. Hop-up. Can be made with the tools listed here; invaluable as a sawing stool, portable bench and platform.
5. 1 m./3 ft folding boxwood rule; 2 or 3 m. (6 or 10 ft) steel tape; try-square; straight-edge (ordinary straight length of timber). This is the basic kit for marking and measuring out.
6. 75 and 150 mm. (3 and 6 in.) screwdrivers; bradawl. For fixing locks and other hardware as well as joinery; a hole made by a bradawl helps entry of screws.
7. Power drill or wheel brace; gimlet. To cope with the basic job of boring holes. A power drill with a masonry bit allows fixing to walls.
8. Abrasive-paper block. Cheap yet invaluable, it is vital for use with abrasive paper to obtain a smooth finish for painting.
9. Tenon saw. For cutting joints, sheet material and to carry out finer work than the panel saw can cope with. It is a better first buy than the panel saw unless you are working on heavier wood most of the time.
10. Smooth plane; combination oilstone. For reducing wood to size and finishing; sharpen the blade frequently on the oilstone.

11. Chisels: 6, 12 and 25 mm. (¼, ½ and 1 in.); 110 mm. (4½ in.) mallet. Firmer chisels are more robust than bevel-edge chisels but are less useful for fine joint cutting—buy the best for your needs.
12. Pliers: 6 in. square-nosed with side cutters. Invaluable for hundreds of pulling, gripping and small wire-cutting jobs.

Looking after tools:
1. Wherever possible, put tools away in a rack when not in immediate use; it can save their being damaged.
2. Keep a piece of oiled felt pad in a shallow tray near the bench so that when tools are finished with, you can rub them over the pad to prevent rust.
3. Never leave tools where children can get hold of them.
4. Always have in stock spare blades for padsaw, coping saw, fretsaw and hacksaw.
5. As soon as you can, make a tool cupboard or chest with a place for everything.

The right tools for the job

Job to be done	Best hand tools		Power tools
Cutting a round hole	Padsaw (or frame saw) File	Drill Compasses	Jig saw Drill
Cutting a square hole	Padsaw Panel saw Drill Straight-edge	Bull-nosed plane Chisel	Jig saw Drill
Screwing into walls	Spirit level Masonry drill Screwdriver Straight-edge	Hammer Chisel	Drill (2 speed)
Removing floor-boards	Nail punch Tenon or panel saw	Claw hammer Wrecking bar	Portable circular saw
Replacing floor-boards	Plane Tenon or panel saw	Hammer Nail punch	
Re-sanding	Floor-scraper Hammer Nail punch Sanding block		Floor sander (hired) Orbital or disc sander
Fitting new door/ new hinges	Tenon saw Marking gauge Chisel Bradawl or drill	Screwdriver Plane	Drill
Fitting new door-lock or latch— simple rim type	Screwdriver Bradawl or drill Padsaw	Brace and bit Small chisel	Drill
Yale type	Above plus expansive bit		
Fitting lock or latch—mortise type	Mortise gauge Brace and bits Padsaw Two chisels Screwdriver		Drill
Fixing handles	Wheel brace and drill	Screwdriver Bradawl	Drill
Fitting simple flush catches	Screwdriver Bradawl or drill		Drill
Timber cladding	Panel saw Tenon saw Claw hammer Nail punch Smooth plane Wide chisel	Coping saw Compasses	Portable circular saw Jig saw

Job to be done	Best hand tools		Power tools
Bird's-mouth joint (for roofing)	Sliding bevel Panel saw Wide chisel		
Box joint (finger joint)	Cutting gauge Marking gauge Small tenon or dovetail saw Coping saw	Chisel (to width of fingers)	Circular saw with special blade and jig Router with jig
Bridle joint	Mortise gauge Wide chisel Narrow chisel	Coping saw Tenon saw	Circular saw Drill
Dovetail halving joint	Marking gauge Tenon saw Chisel Sliding bevel		Router (or circular saw)
Through dovetail Lapped dovetail	Dovetail marker Cutting gauge Marking gauge Dovetail saw Coping saw Tenon saw Smooth plane	Two chisels (to suit size of pins and tails)	
Dowelled joint	Marking gauge Dowel jig Ratchet brace Dowel bit	Depth gauge for bit Hammer	Drill
Halving joint	Marking gauge Chisel Tenon saw		Circular saw
Housing joint (through or stopped)	Marking gauge Tenon saw Hand router	Paring chisel (to suit housing) Chisel	Circular saw (for through housing) Router (for stopped housing)
Mitre joint (with loose tongue)	Mitre square Cutting gauge Tenon saw Smooth (or jack) plane Rough plane	Chisel (to fit groove for tongue)	Router Circular saw
Mortise and tenon joint	Mortise gauge Tenon saw Mortise chisel	Shoulder plane Mallet	Circular saw Drill press mortiser
Rebated joint	Cutting gauge Tenon saw Shoulder plane Smooth plane Marking gauge	Pin hammer	Circular saw Router

Note: a rule, pencil, square and marking knife are essential for almost all the above jobs and are not listed. The list shows which tools to use from a comprehensive kit. Most of the jobs, however, can be done by using tools from the basic tool kit with a few minor additions.

Tools/5

Types of saw

A saw is a succession of cutting edges—teeth—whose size and shape make them suitable for one sort of work and unsuitable for another.

To take extreme examples, a rip saw will not cut a matchstick and a fretsaw will not fell a tree.

The greater the number of teeth, or 'points', a saw blade has per measurement, the finer the cut. Thus a 14 point saw—14 teeth in 25 mm. (1 in.)—cuts finer, though more slowly, than a 10 point saw.

Almost every type of saw has the teeth bent out from the blade, alternate teeth in opposite directions. This is known as 'set', and allows a saw to cut more easily without becoming clogged. It also allows the line of the cut to be adjusted slightly while you work, as the set makes the saw-cut slightly wider than the blade. Accurate set is as important as sharpness.

Despite the wide variety of saws, they can be divided into three main groups, according to the job they do:

1. Big handsaws, for roughly cutting large lengths or sheets of timber to size—panel, cross-cut and rip saws.

2. Saws for cutting joints and other fine and exact work—tenon and dovetail saws.

3. Saws for cutting curves and other special shapes—coping saws, bow saws, padsaws, fretsaws.

Saw handles are usually of plastic or wood. Plastic handles are stronger, but wooden handles are more comfortable to use over long periods as they absorb perspiration better.

Time spent in care and maintenance of your saws prolongs their life. Oil saw blades with light oil to prevent rusting, but wipe off any oil before you start cutting as it will mark the wood.

Lubricate a saw blade in use by rubbing with a candle.

If a blade is rusty, clean it off with steel wool dipped in white spirit.

Do not leave saws lying around on a bench where their teeth may be damaged—hang them upright.

Panel saw

Tenon saw

Coping saw

The versatile panel saw

The panel saw is the best buy for a large all-round handsaw; a suitable size is 560–600 mm. (22–24 in.) long with 10 points.

25 mm. (1 in.)

Panel saw teeth

The panel saw's name is derived from its traditional job of cutting up panels for wardrobe backs, drawer-bottoms and doors, but it cuts large timber generally, both with and across the grain. It is rather slow in ripping boards more than 25 mm. (1 in.) thick. Its teeth are the same as those of a cross-cut saw, but smaller.

Use a panel saw, and other handsaws, with the index finger pointing along the blade for better control. Use the whole length of the blade, applying light pressure on the downward stroke only.

Always make cuts on the waste side of the line you are working to; cutting on the line will leave the wood fractionally undersize, with no scope for planing. Always keep the wood firmly secured—on trestles or similar supports if it is large, in a vice if it is small.

If a large sheet of wood whips when you cut it with a panel saw, rest the sheet on two boards on the trestles and make the cut between the boards.

Plywood and hardboard less than 6 mm. (about $\frac{1}{4}$ in.) thick are best cut with a tenon saw, as a panel saw may tear them.

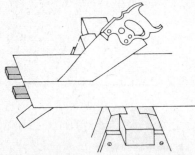

Support whippy sheets on two boards

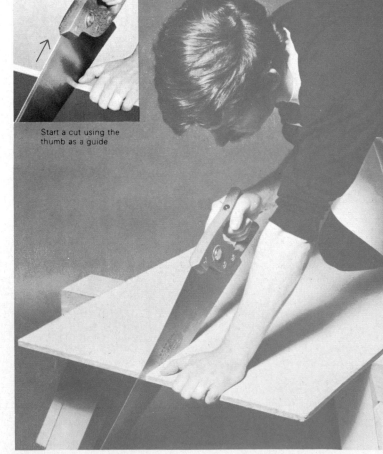

Start a cut using the thumb as a guide

Using a large handsaw. Hold the wood firmly on solid supports with knee and one hand, with your eye over the cut. Start by drawing the saw back just on the waste side of the line, at a shallow angle, using your thumb as a guide.

Rip-sawing

The rip saw is designed for one specific job —cutting timber fast with the grain. It is worth buying if you have a lot of board-ripping to do; if not, use a panel saw.

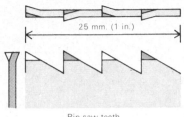

Rip saw teeth

The rip saw's teeth, generally four in 25 mm. (1 in.), are like a series of small chisels. If they cut across the grain they tear out the wood fibres, giving a jagged end. The rip saw works best if the blade is at an angle of about 60° to the wood.

Rip short boards on a single trestle, reversing the wood when the cut gets beyond the half-way mark. Longer work needs two trestles or a couple of chairs. Start cutting at one end, continue between the trestles and finish beyond the second support.

Take care when reaching the end of a long cut that the wood does not snap: if necessary, finish the cut from the end opposite the one from which you started, or cramp a piece of wood across the board to stop it juddering.

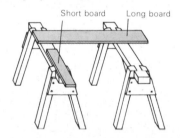

Short board   Long board

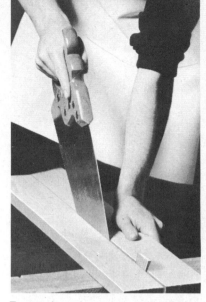

To stop jamming on a long cut, wedge it open with scrap wood as you near the end.

To prevent wandering on awkward grain, cramp on a batten and saw against it.

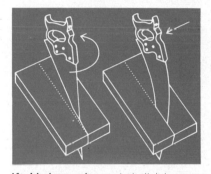

If a blade wanders, twist it slightly as you saw to get back into line. If the blade leaves the vertical, correct it by slight bowing.

Rip overhand when you cannot stand beside the cut. The teeth face away from you and the blade is worked nearly upright.

Cutting across the grain

The cross-cut saw has teeth designed for cutting thick timber across the grain. It leaves a rough finish, however, and is only worth buying if you have a lot of heavy work to do—a panel saw will cope with most cross-cutting quite satisfactorily.

Never saw with the wood between trestles when making a cross-cut, as the wood will bend, jamming the saw, or snap off. Arrange the wood so that the end to be removed overhangs the support. To trim a fraction off the end of a length of wood, cramp a piece of scrap to it, mark lines round both and saw through both pieces at the same time.

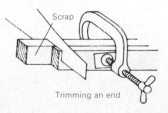

Scrap

Trimming an end

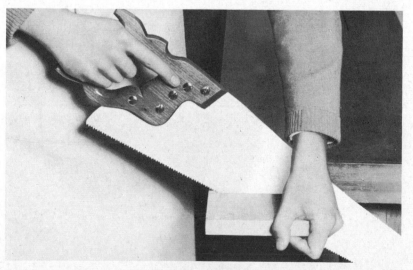

Ending a cross-cut. Avoid splitting the wood by supporting the overhanging end with your free hand as you work. Make the last few strokes gently.

Tenon saw

The steel or brass-backed tenon saw is probably the most useful all-round saw you can have, and should be the first saw you buy.

It is used for nearly all joint-cutting, with and across the grain—with practice you will be able to cut joints with it so that they fit together without further trimming. Its rigid-backed blade also allows accurate cutting of thin sheet material.

For general use, you should buy a 250 or 300 mm. (10 or 12 in.) tenon saw with 14–16 points.

Using a tenon saw can be made easier when cutting across the grain by using a bench hook. This is a simple platform which has a strip of wood at one end that butts against the bench and therefore keeps the bench hook still, and another strip on the reverse side at the other end against which wood is gripped with the hand.

You can easily construct a bench hook at home by using a piece of 18 mm. ($\frac{3}{4}$ in.) hardwood and straight strips which are

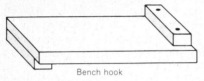

Bench hook

screwed on. Make the platform about 250 × 175 mm. (9 × 7 in.).

To make sure you cut a piece of wood squarely, mark lines on the face side and edge and watch both lines as you cut. Saw on the waste side of the lines and plane

down to them afterwards to get a clean finish.

In cutting mitres, for example to make picture frames, you should use the tenon (or dovetail) saw with a mitre box. For this the wood is held or cramped in the mitre box and the tenon saw is worked through the diagonal guide slots.

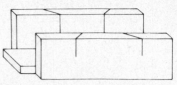

Mitre box

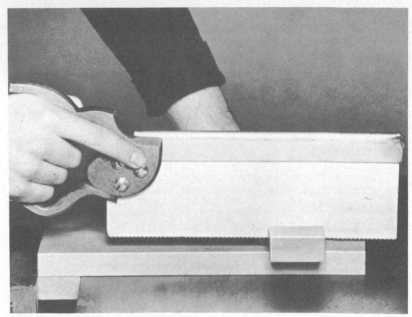

Using a tenon saw. Guide the cut with the index finger. Use the full length of the blade. Keep the wood still, either cramped or, as here, gripped on a bench hook.

To cut a tenon or shoulder, cramp the wood in the vice at an angle so you can see the marking lines on the top and side at the

same time, and saw down just on the waste side of each. Reverse the wood and saw the other side similarly. Cramp the

wood upright in the vice and square off the bottom cut. Finally make the cross-cuts to remove the waste on a bench hook.

Dovetail saw

The dovetail saw, for practical purposes a smaller version of the tenon saw, is used where a finer cut is needed, as on making dovetails. Unlike the tenon saw, its teeth are not set (splayed out alternately). It relies on the burr produced by filing the teeth sharp to give the blade clearance.

The back on a dovetail saw—as on a tenon saw—is either of brass or steel. The object of this back is to give rigidity and weight. Brass is heavier than steel but more expensive and would probably only be the choice of a professional.

Recommended size if buying a dovetail saw: 200 mm. (8 in.) with 18–22 points.

Fine work needs a dovetail saw.

Gents saw

The Gents saw is noteworthy as the smallest member of the backsaw family. It has a straight handle and no set on its teeth. It is most useful as a model-making tool, or for cutting joints in both hardwood and softwood on small work. The smallest size is 100 mm. (4 in.) with a maximum of 32 points. These small saws are usually discarded when blunt but, given good eyesight, you can sharpen the larger ones with a triangular needle-file.

Coping saw

The coping saw is the best all-round saw for curves. It cuts practically any shape, but can saw only as far into the wood as the distance between the blade and the top of the saw frame.

It is versatile enough to tackle jobs ranging from cutting floorboards around pipes to removing waste from dovetails. Cuts can start and finish at the edge of the wood or can be enclosed.

To make an enclosed cut, first drill a hole in the waste part of the wood, thread the blade through the hole and fix it in the frame, then saw to shape.

If you want to cut a grip handle, as shown in the illustration, a better idea is to drill a hole at each end of the waste and saw between them.

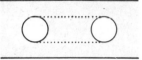

Cutting a grip handle

The coping saw is available in one size only and has replaceable blades which are discarded when blunt, not resharpened. Blades can be bought singly or, more cheaply, in dozens. If buying a coping saw, specify one for woodwork, otherwise you may get a metalwork coping saw on which the blade angle cannot be adjusted.

Blades are fitted on to retaining pins at each side of the frame. The gap between the retaining pins is greater than the length of the blade. When the blade is fitted the natural spring of the frame tensions it and prevents it bending when in use.

To fit a blade, unscrew the handle, allowing the retaining pin to move forward. Hold the frame steady with one hand while pushing the open ends together between the stomach and a firm object, such as a bench, until the blade pegs can be

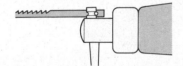

Blade pegs locate in the frame pins

slipped on the retaining pins. The teeth of the blade must point towards the handle so that cutting is done as the saw is drawn through the work.

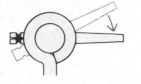

Always keep retaining pins in line

Adjust the blade ready for use by tightening up the handle fully and lining up the retaining pins, to ensure the blade is not twisted.

The coping saw can be used with the blade at an angle to the frame, and cutting a curve is often made easier if you adjust the blade to different angles as you proceed, as shown in the pictures at the foot of this page.

To adjust the blade angle, turn the handle anti-clockwise, enough to loosen the blade, line up the pins so the blade is at the required angle and not twisted, then retighten the handle before continuing to cut.

The coping saw is sometimes used like a fretsaw (see next page). When cutting, always keep your eye on what the blade is doing, not on the 'unnatural' angle of the frame.

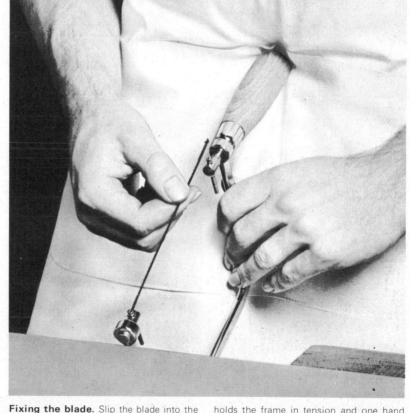

Fixing the blade. Slip the blade into the slots in the retaining pins while the body holds the frame in tension and one hand steadies it. Remove the blade after use.

Cutting a curve. First saw downward, with the frame slightly at an angle so that you can watch the blade, checking that it keeps to the line.

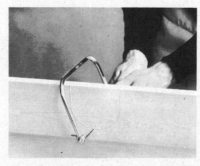

Negotiate the curve deep in the wood by adjusting the blade angle and sawing sideways. Make sure the pins are in line, and the blade not twisted.

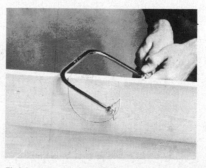

Finish the cut by sawing upward—this will ensure a smoother result than if you make a second cut downward from the top to meet the original cut.

Padsaw

Padsaws cut slowly and are difficult to keep straight, but have the advantage of being able to work where better saws cannot. If you need to cut a hole in the middle of a large panel, for example, the only handsaw that can do the job is a padsaw, working from a drilled hole.

Blades are replaceable and can be bought in a number of lengths. They are clamped in position in the wood or metal handle by tightening a knurled knob or screws. The longer the blade the greater the tendency for it to bend, and although a padsaw blade can be straightened again with the fingers, once it has bent it tends to keep doing so and is therefore best replaced.

Blades can, in theory, be sharpened, but are difficult to hold firmly and it is easier to use a replacement.

Hacksaw blades, for metalworking, can also be fitted into padsaw handles. The commonest use for padsaws is cutting key-holes (hence the alternative name of key-hole saw) and letterboxes.

Keyholes are cut by first drilling a hole, cutting down from it with the padsaw, and clearing out the waste with a chisel. This can be done with a coping saw, but it involves threading and fitting the blade to the frame to make two 6 mm. ($\frac{1}{4}$ in.) cuts.

In cutting a letterbox or similar straight-sided opening, the object is to use the pad-saw as little as possible, because of its limitations.

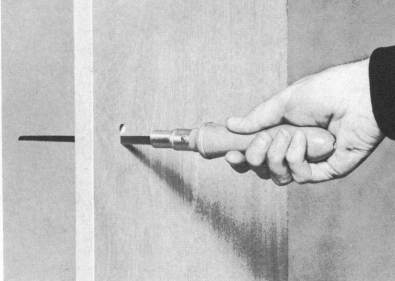

Cutting a keyhole. This is one of the jobs for which a padsaw is ideally suited. Work the saw with one or two hands but take care not to buckle the blade.

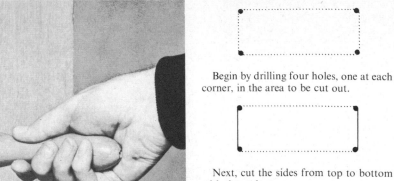

Begin by drilling four holes, one at each corner, in the area to be cut out.

Next, cut the sides from top to bottom with the padsaw.

Finally, start the top and bottom cuts with the padsaw, but as soon as the cuts are long enough, finish off with a panel saw—it is more easily controlled than a padsaw, even when used horizontally.

Bow saw

The bow saw, like the coping saw, cuts curves and special shapes, but its longer, coarser blade allows it to cut faster and to tackle heavier timber. It cannot, however, cut such intricate shapes as the coping saw.

The blade swivels through 360° and its angle is altered by twisting the handle and the knob opposite—do not hold this knob when cutting with the bow saw, it is for adjustment only. Blades are replaceable and are fitted to tapered retaining pins, one at each end of the frame.

To apply tension to the blade, wind the centre wedge round and round until the twine is taut, then slip the wedge down until it is held against the centre crossbar. The teeth of the blade must face away from the handle, to cut on the forward stroke.

Handling a bow saw. Grip the handle in both hands, cut in long easy strokes. Adjust the blade angle as you work to help complete difficult curves.

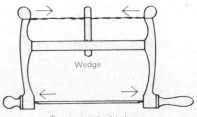

Tensioning the blade

If you lose one of the tapered pins which hold the blade in position, a thin panel pin will serve satisfactorily in its place.

Cramp wood which is to be cut with a bow saw as low in the vice as possible, to stop vibration as you work. This may make it necessary to raise the wood several times during the course of cutting, but will make sawing much easier.

Fretsaw

Model-making is the ideal job for the fret-saw, with its ability to cut intricate curves in thin ply. Fit blades with the teeth facing downward, and cut only on the downward stroke. The blade angle is not adjustable as the blades are fine enough to take curves without being turned.

Cut on the line with a fretsaw, as the cut is smooth enough to require no further trimming. Never force the blade so that it bends while cutting.

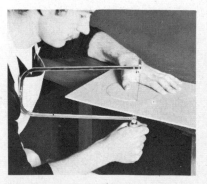

Sit down to use a fretsaw, holding the work flat on a table top or a special model-making table with a cut-out V, over which the work is placed for cutting.

Sharpening saws

A sharp, well-set saw is essential for fast, easy cutting. You can send a saw away to a toolshop for sharpening, or you can learn to do the job yourself, saving time and money.

Make your first attempt at sharpening on a fairly new saw, because the angles of its teeth will still be easy to see.

You need two triangular files—150 mm. (6 in.) for panel and other large saws, and 75 or 100 mm. (3 or 4 in.) for tenons and dovetails—and a saw set to ensure that the angle at which the teeth are bent out from the blade will be constant.

The sharpening method is much the same for all wood saws. The object is to file the worn teeth to a point by removing as little metal as possible.

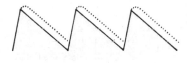

Bringing teeth to a point

First, support the saw in a vice with a hardwood strip either side, so it is held firmly throughout its length. Shape the strips with a coping saw to fit round the handle. Cramp the blocks in the vice with the teeth just protruding.

Alternatively you can make a simple saw-sharpening trestle. Such a trestle holds the saw at a more convenient height for sharpening.

Start filing from the handle end on the first tooth bent away from you.

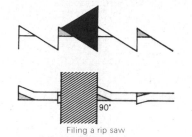

Filing a rip saw

For a rip saw, hold the file horizontally and at right angles to the blade. For a cross-cut, panel, tenon or dovetail saw, hold the file in a horizontal position at about 60° to the blade.

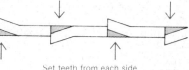

Filing a cross-cut or panel saw

Use the original sharpening angle as your guide and stroke the tooth firmly two or three times with the file.

The tooth is sharp when it gleams right up to the point. Move on to the next tooth but one, and then continue along the blade, sharpening every tooth set away from you. Reverse the saw and repeat the process.

Stop filing the instant worn points disappear, otherwise you will skim off too much metal.

The next stage is the setting. Fix the saw higher up in the hardwood blocks before you start.

Adjust the graduated dial on the saw set so that the figure at the top corresponds to the number of teeth in 25 mm. (1 in.) on the saw. You may prefer to use a higher number, giving a finer setting, if you use the saw mainly for hardwoods.

Set teeth from each side

Set every alternate tooth, then reverse the saw and set the remaining ones. The saw set is used in the same way as a pair of pliers, fitting over the tooth which is set by a squeeze of the handles.

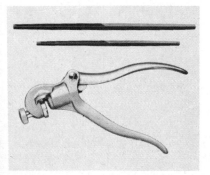

Tools needed. Triangular files and a saw set, which presses the teeth on to a graduated anvil, giving the correct angle.

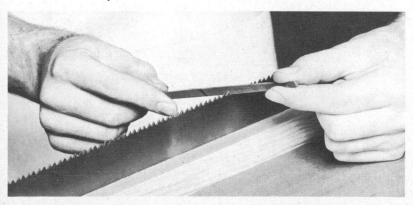

Ready for filing. Support the saw in hardwood strips. Long saws may need to be cramped at each end to keep them rigid. If the teeth are not level, smooth them by running a smooth file the length of the blade before filing.

How to file. Hold the file at each end and place it in the V in front of the tooth's cutting edge. File only the angled cutting edges if you are working on a fairly new saw that just needs touching up. If the teeth are well worn, file deeper into the V in order to restore the points. Use only light strokes of the file.

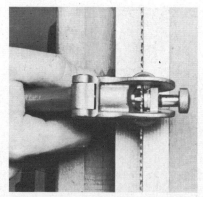

Setting. The number showing at the top of the saw set should equal the saw's teeth in 25 mm. (1 in.). Set every alternate tooth, reversing the saw to set the rest.

Tools/11

Metal planes

Planes come in a multitude of patterns to cope with special jobs. The basic planing job, however, is to reduce wood to exact dimensions, leaving it smooth and flat.

Three sorts of metal plane do this: the jointer plane 550–600 mm. (22–24 in.) long; the jack plane 350–375 mm. (14–15 in.); and the smooth plane 200–250 mm. (8–10 in.). The longer the plane the flatter it cuts a surface, since a short plane 'rides' the bumps instead of straddling them. The best all-round plane is the jack, as it is long enough to cope with most surfaces and is not as heavy as the jointer plane.

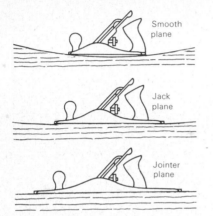

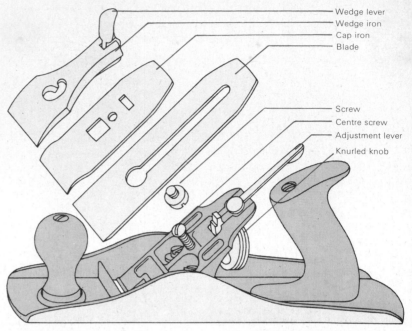

Wedge lever
Wedge iron
Cap iron
Blade

Screw
Centre screw
Adjustment lever
Knurled knob

Smooth plane

Jack plane

Jointer plane

Familiarise yourself with the different parts of your plane and their functions, as you need to adjust the plane before use and to take it apart to sharpen the blade.

To remove the blade, lift the wedge lever and slide the wedge out; remove the blade

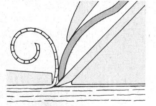

A well-adjusted cap iron cracks shavings, to give an even cut

and cap iron and release the screw so that they slide apart. After the blade is sharpened (see p. 17) screw the blade and cap iron together tightly, so that the cap iron is about 1·5 mm. ($\frac{1}{16}$ in.) back from the cutting edge, and parallel with it—this is vital for smooth cutting.

Replace the blade and cap iron—the blade's bevel face downward—and the wedge iron, then depress the lever. If the whole assembly is loose, tighten the centre screw slightly. If the lever will not depress, then the assembly is not in correctly.

Adjust the depth of cut by turning the knurled knob, which controls how far the blade sticks out of the slot, then adjust the blade so that it will cut evenly across its full width.

Longer-lasting tungsten-tipped blades used in certain planes must be sent away for regrinding when blunt.

Some metal planes use replaceable blades that are thrown away when blunt. They are released, and new ones are secured, by the simple operation of a cam lever.

Adjusting the blade. Look along the plane bottom and make the blade parallel with it by moving the adjustment lever.

Wooden planes

Wooden planes are less common than metal ones, but are available in three sizes—trying plane, jack and smooth—equivalent to the three basic metal ones.

Adjusting them for use takes practice. Remove the blade, cap iron and wedge by holding them in one hand, turning the plane upside down and rapping its front end on the bench. To reassemble, hold the blade and cap iron in place with the thumb and tap the wedge in with a hammer. Align the blade by tapping with the hammer, ending with a firm tap on the cap iron and the wedge so that the whole assembly is firm. To make minor readjustments, loosen the assembly by tapping the top front end of the plane—often there is a domed knob there for this purpose.

To prevent drying out, wipe wooden planes occasionally with raw linseed oil.

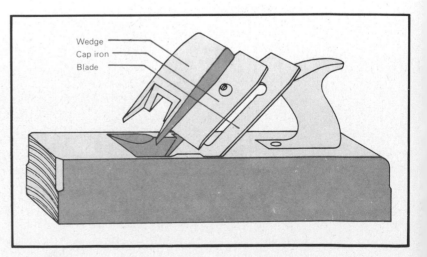

Wedge
Cap iron
Blade

Planing tips

Always sharpen and adjust a plane before using it. Check the wood for nails if it is not new. Strip painted wood, otherwise the plane blade will not be able to bite.

Support the wood so that it will stay perfectly still as you work: put long wood on a flat surface against a stop; if your bench top is not level, use a stout, level board with a stop screwed on the end.

To plane end grain, put the wood as low down in the vice as you can so that it will not vibrate, or use a shooting board. Check edges for square frequently as you work, with a try-square. Check that long wood is level by looking along it frequently. Plane off raised areas before finally planing the whole board.

Plane towards knots from either side if the grain of the wood is very rough.

Lubricate the bottom of the plane when in use by rubbing with a candle end. Wipe any resin from the wood off the bottom of the plane, as it makes planing harder work.

After use, store planes on their sides in a dry place, clearing away shavings and sawdust, which attract damp and cause the cutting edge to rust. Wipe all exposed metal with an oily rag.

Planing long wood. Press down on the front of the plane at the start of the stroke, easing up until as you finish the pressure is on the back. Try to produce ribbon-like shavings. Work with the wood on a flat surface, with the end against a stop.

Planing long edges. Guide with the front hand, fingers brushing against the wood, thumb pressing downward. Make the stroke the length of the wood.

Chamfering. Use the fingers and the thumb of the front hand as a guide, as with planing a long edge. Keep the elbow of the rear arm well in for greater stability.

End grain. Avoid splitting off end grain by cutting off a corner and planing towards it. Alternatively, plane towards the centre from each end of the wood in turn.

Making a shooting board

A shooting board, used with the jointer or jack plane, makes for accuracy in end-grain work. It should also be used for planing the long-grain edge of thin panels.

It basically consists of two boards which guide the plane, and a 90° stop against which to hold the work.

A shooting board can be made at home, preferably out of beech. Make sure the wood is not warped and that the stop is dead square; a length of 900 mm. (3 ft) is about right.

A mitre shooting board has a stop set at 45° to where the plane runs, and is invaluable when making picture frames.

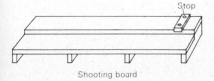

Shooting board

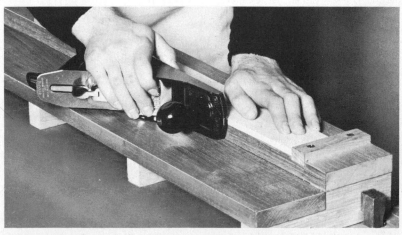

Using the board. Hold the plane on its side against the guide pieces. If the wood you are planing is thicker than the stop, insert a spare strip between them to prevent the plane from splitting the end grain on the otherwise unprotected top corner.

Block plane

Used with one or two hands, the block plane is useful for small work and for end-grain trimming, to which it is particularly suited because of its shallow blade-angle.

The blade, 35–41 mm. (1⅜–1⅝ in.) wide, is controlled for depth by a nut under the handle, and for side adjustment by the projecting lever. It cuts bevel uppermost. The mouth opening on some makes also adjusts for coarse or fine shavings.

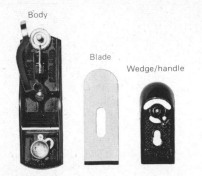

Use it one-handed for chamfering—pressing with the forefinger on the button at the front—and two-handed for end-grain work.

Trimming end grain. Use the block plane with the left thumb and forefinger guiding the front and keeping it level. Cup the right hand round the body of the plane. Trim from each end to the middle to avoid splitting the far corner.

Moulding plane

Moulding planes are specialist tools for forming and smoothing shaped edges. Planes for cutting a variety of shapes, both convex and concave, are available. The shape cut by a moulding plane can be altered by regrinding its blade and planing the body to match. Blades are removed and fixed by tapping the wedge, and sharpened by using a slipstone on the ground side and a flat stone on the back. Before using a moulding plane, chamfer off as much waste as possible with a flat-bottomed plane.

Blade   Wedge   Plane body

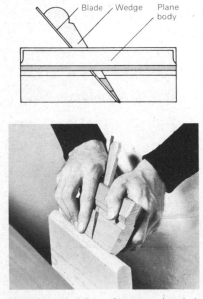

Use the moulding plane two-handed. The fingers of one hand should just be touching the timber as you work, as a guide.

Shoulder plane

The shoulder plane is chiefly used for trimming up shoulders/tenons and rebates. The blade cuts the full width of the plane body so that it can trim right into the angle.

There are two types—the traditional wooden pattern and the modern all-metal type with a screw-adjusted blade.

Another version has a detachable fore section which, when removed, enables you to work close up to internal corners, as with a bullnose plane.

When cutting a rebate, cramp a straight-edged length of wood along the line of the cut as a guide to the plane. Keep the side of the plane pushed in against the guide as you work.

Tenons and shoulders in cabinet work are cleaned up with the shoulder plane. Work in from the edges to the centre to avoid splitting the wood.

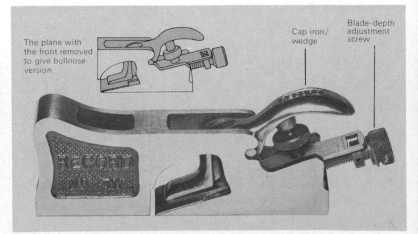

Two-in-one plane. This version of the shoulder plane also doubles as a bullnose, capable of working right up to an internal corner. The blade is removed from the plane through the bottom and is sharpened like an ordinary plane iron.

Rebate plane

The rebate or fillister plane cuts rebates for glass or panelling.

There are two blade positions. Use the standard centre position for all normal open-ended rebating on the bench; use the bullnose position for stopped rebates or for cutting or enlarging rebates in an existing frame.

To cut a rebate running up to a vertical surface, chisel out enough at the fore end of the work to allow the plane to run through in its bullnose setting.

Work the plane in progressive stages: start from the front end with a series of short cuts, gradually stepping backwards until you have the entire rebate. This method prevents the plane wandering with the grain away from the side of the rebate.

Arrange the work so that the plane never comes up against opposing grain. If you are in doubt about the slope of the grain, a trial shaving will indicate the direction—the plane will dig into and tear opposing grain.

Making the cut in stages

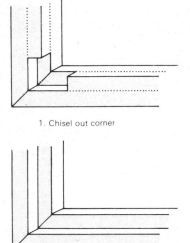

1. Chisel out corner

2. Plane up to chisel cuts to complete the rebate

The plane has an adjustable side-fence which controls the width of the rebate, and a gauge for depth.

The blades cut bevel down. Adjust the cutting edge with the lever behind the blade.

Cup the left hand comfortably round the fence rod and body of the plane, keeping it pressed well into the work. Push forward and down with the right hand.

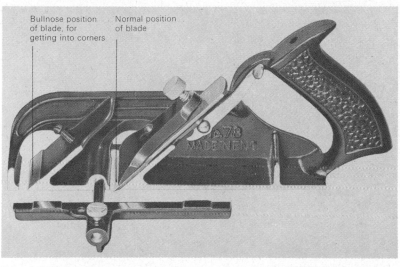

Bullnose position of blade, for getting into corners

Normal position of blade

Set the blade in the standard centre position for normal bench work. Use it in the bullnose position for stopped rebates and for working close to vertical surfaces.

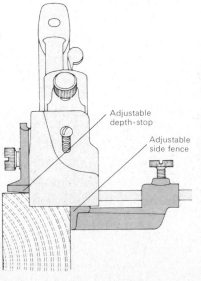

Adjustable depth-stop

Adjustable side fence

Front view of rebate plane

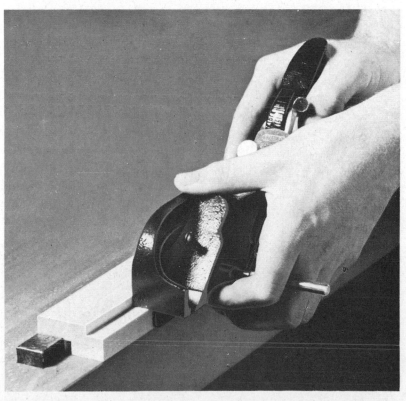

The plane in use, cutting a rebate. Guide the plane with the front hand, holding the plane into the wood. Care must be taken to keep the plane upright

Tools/15

Types of chisels

Your first set of chisels should be of the bevel-edge type. They will do most chiselling jobs and have the advantage of being able to 'undercut'—get into tight corners—because of their tapered edges. Buy four to start with, say 6, 12, 18 and 25 mm. ($\frac{1}{4}$, $\frac{1}{2}$, $\frac{3}{4}$ and 1 in.).

Firmer chisels, which have blades of rectangular cross-section, are stronger and so better for heavier work such as fence-building and large frame construction.

The paring chisel can be of either blade pattern. Its blade is for paring out long housings, as on bookcases and stairs.

The mortise chisel is the stoutest of all, being designed to withstand the continual striking with a mallet to chop mortises.

When you buy any of these chisels, check that the blades are of the size stated (they often vary slightly). Note that chisel backs are flat in width only, and slightly 'arched' in length.

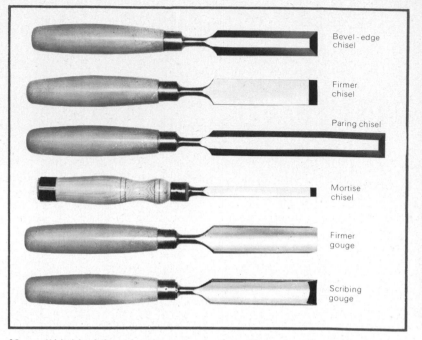

Bevel-edge chisel

Firmer chisel

Paring chisel

Mortise chisel

Firmer gouge

Scribing gouge

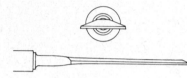

Blades are flat across, arched in length

Chisels are never sharp when first bought, and the first thing to do with a new chisel is to hone the back flat for at least

35 mm. ($1\frac{1}{2}$ in.) back from the cutting edge. The flatness shows up as a bright smooth area, and it must extend over the total width of the blade and right up to the cutting edge, otherwise the blade will never become sharp. This operation may take

about 15 minutes; after completing it, the chisel should be honed as shown on p. 82.

Gouges are of two types: the firmer with its bevel on the back, and the far more useful scribing type with the bevel on the inside face.

Using chisels

Chisels are mainly used for paring, joint cutting or for cutting out small areas of wood to receive hinges or other fittings.

Always use a chisel with or across the grain. Cutting against the grain usually splits the timber or causes the chisel to run off the intended line.

When driving a chisel into wood, as in cutting a mortise or removing the waste from a dovetail joint, always cut well within the waste area first, gradually working up to the marking-out lines for the final cut. If you start a cut on the line, the chisel will overshoot it as you drive it in. Make final cuts with the wedge of the chisel facing the waste area.

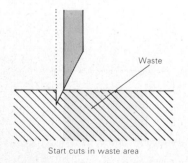

Start cuts in waste area

When mortises have to be cut near the end of a piece of wood, as with a table leg, the wedge action of the chisel tends to break off the wood at the end. To prevent this, leave some waste at the end of the

wood, cut the mortise, and then trim the wood to size.

When cleaning out undercuts, such as a dovetail section, a square-edged firmer chisel will not reach right into the corners—use a bevel-edge chisel, which is specially made for the purpose.

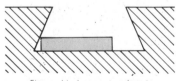

Firmer chisels cannot undercut

Chopping out the waste from a dovetail joint calls for a narrow chisel to remove all but the last 1·5 mm. ($\frac{1}{16}$ in.) of the waste in front of the marking-out line. This last cut is made on the line with a chisel matching the width of the final cut as closely as possible. Drive the chisel in squarely.

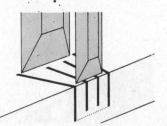

Use two chisels for dovetail-cutting

Using gouges

Use a firmer gouge to cut shallow indents and curved grooves, and a scribing gouge to trim curves to match a mating surface.

When using a firmer gouge, work from each end alternately towards the middle until you reach the required depth.

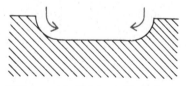

Work from each side when cutting hollows

The sort of job a scribing gouge is used for is fitting a rail to a round leg on a chair or table.

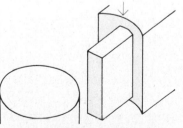

Shape this edge with a scribing gouge

Only buy gouges as the need arises—the firmer gouge is the least used of all the chisel family. Note that gouges are always graded on the width of the blade, never on the radius of the cut.

Oilstones and slipstones

The first essential for sharpening is an oilstone. Oilstones are made in three grades of grit: coarse, medium and fine. Combination stones have sides of two different grades, usually medium and fine. Sizes are $152 \times 50 \times 25$ mm. ($6 \times 2 \times 1$ in.) or $203 \times 50 \times 25$ mm. ($8 \times 2 \times 1$ in.). The longer the stone the more effective each sharpening stroke will be.

Coarse stones are for removing large amounts of steel. They are not generally needed for home sharpening but are useful for removing a chipped cutting edge. Never use them on the flat backs of blades.

Medium grade stones cut more finely than coarse ones, but do not give a good cutting edge. This grade is usually used after grinding and before the fine stone.

Fine stones are used for giving the final cutting edge to a blade. Your stone should have at least one fine side.

Keep and use your oilstone in a homemade hardwood box with a matching lid.

To make the box, mortise a slot in the wood the same width as the stone, 12 mm. ($\frac{1}{2}$ in.) deep, and the length of the stone plus 18 mm. ($\frac{3}{4}$ in.). Cut two pieces of the hardest and closest end-grain wood you can

find to pack out each end of the stone in the box, making them flush with the stone's top. These prevent damage to blades which run off the stone and, by allowing the full length of the stone to be used, reduce chances of uneven wear. Drive four panel pins into the base of the box and cut them off so the ends just protrude; these stop the box slipping when in use on the bench. Make the slot in the lid slightly larger all round than the stone.

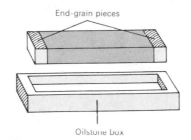

End-grain pieces

Oilstone box

Slipstones are smaller and often finer than oilstones. They are used for sharpening less common tools, including gouges. Unlike oilstones, they are held in the hand and rubbed over the tool which is being

sharpened. The four basic shapes are triangular, round, rectangular and the gouge stone, which is tapered to give two curves of different radii.

Slipstone shapes

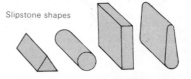

Keep slipstones in their own box, away from workshop dust, or in paraffin.

Never use an oilstone without lightly oiling it first; white spirit can be used if you run out of oil, provided the stone is treated gently. When sharpening, make use of the whole surface of the stone and do not run in one place all the time.

If a stone is worn hollow, regrind it flat with silver sand (as used in bird cages) and a sheet of old glass. Sprinkle the glass with sand and rub the stone over it with a rotary action. Keep the stone dampened with water as you rub. Continue rubbing until the stone is flat and clean all over.

If a stone is oil-clogged, drain it by putting it in a tray in a warm oven.

Honing chisels and plane blades

Chisels and plane blades have two angles forming their cutting edge, the ground angle of 25° and the honed angle of 30°.

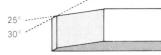

Chisel's ground and honed angles

The ground angle is formed on a grindstone and only needs occasional renewing. The honed angle is formed and maintained by rubbing on an oilstone to give a razor-sharp edge. To hone a chisel or plane blade, oil the stone then hold the blade at an angle of about 30° to the stone, rubbing it to and fro the length of the stone until a burr is built up all along the flat side of the cutting edge—you can feel this by running your thumb along it. Get the blade at the correct angle to the stone either by resting the ground angle on the stone then raising the back end up slightly, or by using a honing guide into which the blade fixes ready for rubbing.

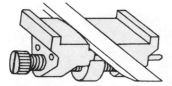

Honing guide—a variable slot for the blade

When the burr has built up on the flat side, rub that from side to side on the stone until the burr turns back. The blade must be kept flat on the stone all the time you are doing this.

Continue rubbing each side of the edge on the stone in turn, using less and less

pressure each time. The burr is thus being bent one way, then the other, getting thinner each time until it falls off, leaving a razor-sharp edge, which should cut a hanging sheet of paper.

Some chisels may not retain an edge for more than a few minutes' work; better-quality chisels will last much longer. In any case, check that blades are sharp before using them, and hone if necessary.

When honing the angled side of the cutting edge, keep the blade's sides parallel with those of the stone. Plane blades which

are wider than the oilstone are held at an angle across the stone, then worked to and fro in the same way as chisels.

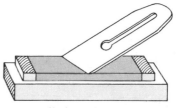

Honing a wide blade

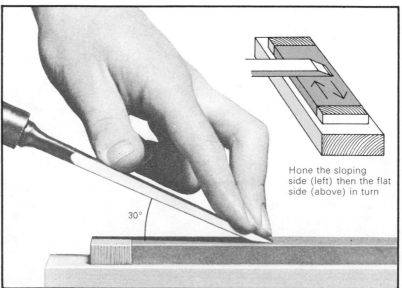

Hone the sloping side (left) then the flat side (above) in turn

30°

Take care to keep the blade at a constant angle of 30° as you rub the honed angle to and fro along the stone—use two hands to hold the blade or buy a honing guide. When rubbing the flat side, keep the blade flat on the stone as you work.

How to hone gouges

The sharpening procedure of obtaining a burr on the cutting edge, then wearing it thinner and thinner until it drops off, applies to gouges as much as to any other chisel. The method for gouges only differs in the way the blade is rubbed and the type of stone used. Gouges, like flat chisels, have two angles at the cutting edge.

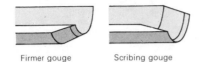

Firmer gouge   Scribing gouge

With firmer gouges, the burr is built up on the inside of the curved edge first, by honing the outer, angled face on a flat stone in a series of sideways, twisting actions which allows all the edge to come equally into contact with the stone.

When the burr is built up on the inside edge, it is reversed by honing with a slipstone, which must be kept flat along the blade's length. This two-fold process is repeated until the burr drops off.

The scribing gouge is sharpened similarly but in reverse sequence: the angled edge on the inside is honed with the slipstone at 30° to the blade, the burr being built up on the convex back of the blade and turned back by rubbing from side to side on a flat stone with a twisting action. The back of the blade must be held flat on the stone while this is being done.

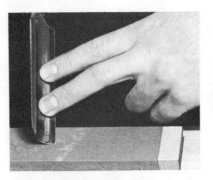
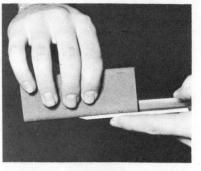

Firmer gouges. First build up a burr by rubbing the angled side of the blade on the oilstone, using a twisting action. Return the burr by rubbing to and fro with a slipstone. Be sure to build up and return the burr all along the cutting edge.

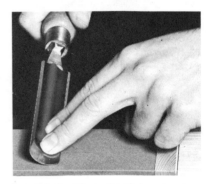

Scribing gouges. First use the slipstone to build up a burr by rubbing the angled cutting edge with the stone at 30°. Rub from side to side on the oilstone to return the burr. The blade must be kept flat on the stone as you twist it from side to side.

How to regrind

When blades become gapped or curved at the cutting edge as a result of a lot of honing, they should be reground; that is, have the blade squared up and the ground angle of 25° restored.

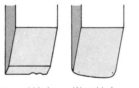

Gapped blade   Worn blade

Regrinding gouges should be left to a tool merchant as the process is tricky. Chisels and plane blades can be done at home, however, either by rubbing on a coarse oilstone (which is hard work) or by means of a grinding wheel.

Electrically-powered grinders are better than hand-worked wheels, as the power model, among other advantages, leaves both hands free to hold the blade being reground (see p. 61).

To regrind a blade, first check that the cutting edge is at right angles to the sides, using a try-square. If it is not, or if the cutting edge is nicked or gashed, grind it back square by touching it on the wheel.

To restore the ground angle, rest the blade on a tool rest at the correct angle and touch it lightly against the wheel. Do not let the blade overheat—keep it cool by dipping it in water between grinding. If the cutting edge turns blue, it has lost temper and will be impossible to sharpen. If this happens, you must grind off the blued areas and start again.

Move wide plane blades from side to side across the wheel as you regrind, so that the whole of the edge is properly ground. As a check that a blade is ground correctly, measure the length of the ground face; it should be $2\frac{1}{2}$ times the thickness of the blade.

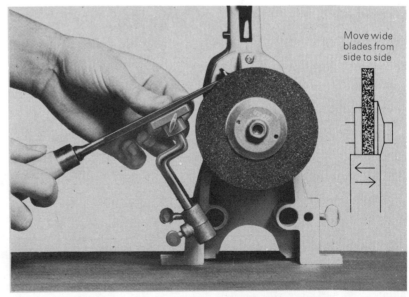

Move wide blades from side to side

The grindstone must revolve downward towards the cutting edge as you work. Touch the blade lightly against the wheel as too much pressure burns the edge. Grinding will leave a slightly hollow edge which must be honed before use.

Cutting a housing

Cut housings (slots across the grain) with the wood securely cramped down so that it will not move as you work, and you have two hands free to use the chisel. Guide the blade with one hand and push with the other. Work with the blade bevel upward.

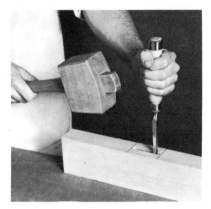

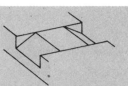
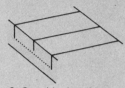
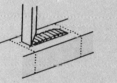

1. Mark out the width on the top and the width and depth on both sides of the wood.

2. Saw down just inside the vertical lines, as far as the depth lines.

3. Chisel out waste a little at a time from both sides, cutting upward.

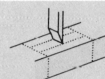
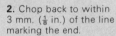
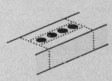

4. Pare away the central waste until you reach the bottom.

5. Shave the bottom so that it is smooth. Check for flatness with a rule.

6. On wider housings, make extra saw-cuts in the waste to facilitate chiselling.

Cutting a mortise

Use a beech mallet to hit the chisel for mortising. Use a chisel the exact width of the planned mortise, which should be not more than one-third of the wood's thickness. The chisel's sides must always be at right angles to the surface of the wood.

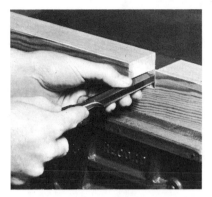

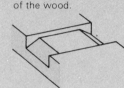
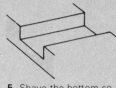
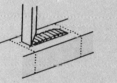

1. Drive the chisel into the centre of the mortise, loosening a wedge of waste.

2. Chop back to within 3 mm. ($\frac{1}{8}$ in.) of the line marking the end.

3. Chop out in the opposite direction from the first cut.

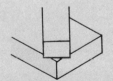
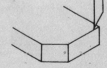
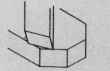

4. Remove waste and continue chopping to the required depth. Cut a through mortise from both sides of the wood.

5. Remove the last 3 mm. of waste from each end of the mortise.

6. As an alternative, drill out the waste and clean up with a chisel.

How to pare

Keep your head over the work, and the chisel upright. Work on a smooth surface —not directly on the bench top. Hold the chisel with the right hand at the top, the thumb giving downward thrust.

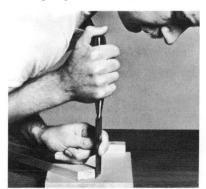

1. To pare a curve, first cut off one corner at about 45°.

2. Cut the other corner.

3. Pare off the corners left by the first cuts.

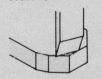

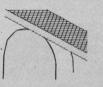

4. Continue cutting off corners, keeping the chisel upright.

5. Work in as close to the line of the curve as possible.

6. Finish off the curve by smoothing with a file.

Drawing knife

The drawing knife is one of the simplest of the shaping tools—basically it is just a blade between two handles—and now perhaps the least-used. It is for removing large amounts of wood from broad surfaces to form flats or curves, where it would be tough going with the more delicate spokeshave.

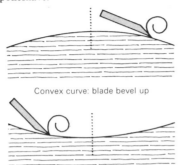

Convex curve: blade bevel up

Concave curve: blade bevel down

It is invaluable for such jobs as shaping heavy timber as used in some garden furniture, or for cutting wide chamfers on beams. It is a tricky tool to use, but with practice it can be very accurate.

Tackle flat or convex shapes with the flat side of the blade nearest to the work. For concave shapes, use the tool the other way up.

Grasp the two handles firmly and press the thumbs on to the corners formed by the tangs. Thumb pressure is quite important in controlling the cutting angle of the blade. As with the spokeshave, work from the middle on convex shapes and from each end on concave shapes.

A big advantage of this knife is that it can work right up to any obstruction.

The blade can be 250 or 300 mm. (10 or 12 in.) long. Sharpening procedure is similar to that for chisels, except that the oilstone is drawn over the blade, not the blade over the stone. Hone the bevelled edge first to achieve a burr, then hone the flat back to reverse it; continue honing each side of the blade in turn until the burr drops off.

Place drawing knife firmly on bench when honing it with a hand-held oilstone.

Thumb pressure controls the cutting angle of the knife, which is drawn, not pushed.

Surforms

Surforms are light, easy-to-handle shaping tools with replaceable, open rasp-like blades. They come in a variety of shapes, including types with curved blades and circular ones for enlarging holes.

These tools shape most materials which are softer than metal, but give a rough finish which may need fining down with sandpaper. There are two ways of using the Surform. For fast work, hold it at an angle to the wood so that the actual cutting edges of the teeth meet the grain square on. For a smoother finish use the Surform with a straighter action so that the teeth themselves cut at an angle.

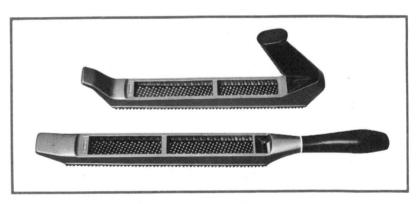

Rasps

The rasp is another shaping tool available in a great variety of types. The finish it gives depends on the fineness of the teeth, but wood generally needs sanding after using a rasp on it.

A 250 mm. (10 in.) long, half-round rasp is suitable for general use. It can tackle almost any shape in wood, ply, hardboard, plastic and even soft metals.

Handles are bought separately and simply knocked on to the spike.

Use it with both hands, one on the handle, the other on the end of the blade.

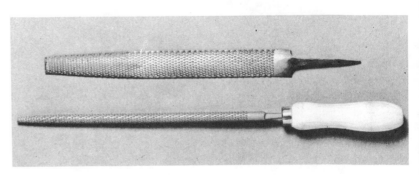

Softwoods

Softwood is timber from coniferous trees with needle-like leaves. Yew is classified as a softwood, although it is harder than many hardwoods.

Softwood can be bought either sawn or planed. Sawn timber is rough, as it comes straight from being cut up without further finishing. Because of shrinkage, sawn timber may be fractionally smaller than the size by which it is sold.

Planed timber is machined smooth for final cleaning up at home. The machining cuts down its dimensions, so that a piece sold as 25×150 mm. (1×6 in.), for instance, will be approximately 22×147 mm. ($\frac{7}{8} \times 5\frac{3}{4}$ in.).

If the exact size is vital, order planed timber to 'finished size'. A 25×100 mm. piece would be planed from the next standard size up (32×150 mm.). This would obviously affect the price.

When buying timber, it is always better to go to the timber yard and examine the timber before accepting it than to order by telephone.

Softwoods other than western red cedar may deteriorate extremely quickly outdoors and must be protected with preservative fluids or paints.

For rafters and joists, order softwood chemically impregnated against rot and woodworm. Planed softwoods used for floors, walls and ceilings need protection against becoming ingrained with dirt—a clear lacquer finish will give this and will let the natural colour of the wood show through.

Many softwoods, particularly redwood and whitewood, have a high resin content, which is often seen as hard brown pockets that weep with sticky syrup-like liquid. Cut out large areas, and seal knots and tiny pockets with knotting which can be obtained at most paint and do-it-yourself shops, before priming and painting.

Splits in the ends of boards are quite common and allowance should be made for them when buying. On large jobs, allow at least 5–10 per cent waste to cover these faults.

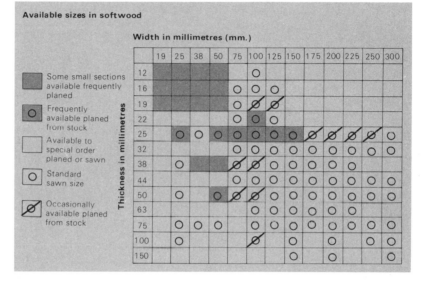

Available sizes in softwood

- ▇ Some small sections available frequently planed
- ⊘(grey) Frequently available planed from stock
- ☐ Available to special order planed or sawn
- O Standard sawn size
- Ø Occasionally available planed from stock

Width in millimetres (mm.) / Thickness in millimetres (mm.)

Thickness \ Width	19	25	38	50	75	100	125	150	175	200	225	250	300
12						O							
16					O	O	O						
19					O	Ø	Ø						
22					O	O	O						
25	O	O	O	O	O	O	O	O	Ø	Ø	Ø	Ø	O
32					O	O	O	O	O	O	O	O	O
38	O			Ø	Ø	Ø	O	O	O	O	O	O	O
44					O	Ø	O	O	O	O	O	O	O
50	O			O	Ø	Ø	O	O	O	O	O	O	O
63						O	O	O	O	O	O		
75		O	O	O		O	O	O	O	O	O	O	O
100		O				Ø		O		O		O	O
150								O		O			O

Hardwoods

Hardwoods are basically timbers for furniture making. They are more expensive than softwoods but more resistant to surface marking; and they have a longer life than softwoods.

Do not be afraid to use hardwoods. As long as your tools are keen-edged, these woods can be cut, turned and jointed better than softwoods.

Hardwood moves less than softwood, and gives a better fit when jointed. Its decorative effect is superior, too, because it takes a better surface finish.

Home-grown hardwoods are sometimes a little more difficult to work than smooth-textured imported ones. English oak, for example, is usually harder to work than Japanese.

Most timber yards stock imported hardwoods in square-edged sawn boards. English timbers usually have at least one waney edge. Hardwood suppliers will

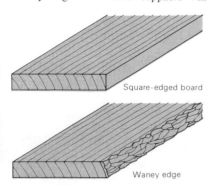

Square-edged board

Waney edge

usually saw or plane to any size required, but generally a few days must be allowed for this to be done.

A rule with most hardwoods is to avoid sapwood and the heart centre of the log. Sapwood is much softer than wood of the established growth; and the heart usually splits, shrinks or twists.

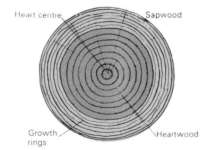

Heart centre — Sapwood
Growth rings — Heartwood

The standard thicknesses of sawn hardwoods are 19, 22, 25, 32, 38, 50, 75 and 100 mm. Widths depend on the size of the tree, but many imported square-edged boards are cut to 150, 175, 200 and 225 mm.

In planing, up to 3 mm. is lost from both the nominal width and thickness (as with softwoods), but teak is usually an exception to this rule. A teak board quoted as being 25 mm. (1 in.) thick in the sawn state, for example, sometimes measures 28 or 29 mm. ($1\frac{1}{8}$ or $1\frac{3}{16}$ in.), so that, with care, the finished size when planed will hold up to 25 mm.

Look for timber that has been properly stacked. The usual methods with home-grown hardwoods is to stack the boards as they come from the logs. If the stack is untidy, it probably means that someone has sorted through the boards and rejected those that are left.

The quality of hardwood depends greatly on the way it has been seasoned and stored. The best method of storing is known as stick-drying, and it is worth looking to see if this method is used in your local timber yard.

A through and through sawn log in stick drying.

Try to buy from the oldest log, which is often the dirtiest, rather than clean-looking timber that is probably fresh. Home-grown woods should stand under cover in this 'sticked' state for three or four years before use.

When timber is badly dried or not cared for while it is in stick, there is a danger that water will collect around the sticks and cause permanent stick marks well into the boards.

The ends of boards dry out more quickly than the centres, and this causes fairly long, wide cracks. To reduce risk of this, some boards are pitched or painted at the ends to seal the grain.

Woods/2

Plywood

Plywood is made from an odd number of constructional veneers, bonded face to face, with the grain running in alternate directions.

The greater the number of veneers, the stronger the plywood. The reason for using an odd number of veneers is that the sheet of plywood must be balanced as near as possible to be stable.

The balancing works like this:

If two veneers, A and B, are bonded together, tensions created by the glue line, and inherent in the veneers themselves, will cause warping.

By using two B veneers, bonded one on each side of A, the tensions are equalised. This is basic 3-ply.

New veneers are added in pairs, one on each side, keeping the balance and building up to 11 plies or more.

There can be no 2-, 4-, 6-, 8- or 10-ply because this would warp.

Plywood can still twist—and sometimes does—even when it is balanced, because no two veneers are completely identical and the tensions are never perfectly balanced. Another factor that can cause warping is the wetting or heating of one face of the ply; this will cause the veneer to expand or contract, both of which can pull the board out of true.

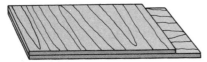

Two veneers bonded together . . .

will warp like this

Three will remain relatively stable

Ply for special jobs

If the finished piece is to be used outside or in damp conditions, you will need ply laminated with a waterproof bond. Ask for Exterior WBP, which is waterproof and boilproof. For boat-building, you need marine ply, specification BS 1088; for shuttering, use WBP ply with a phenolic resin coating.

Face veneered ply
Plywood is available in a number of thicknesses, with decorative hardwood face veneers. Plastic-laminated plywood (the best known is Beautyboard) is available.

Ply timbers
Most plywood is imported, and the more common types are: birch, Gaboon and West African mahogany, beech, Parana pine and Douglas fir.

Birch ply. One of the strongest plywoods, it has a tendency to twist if poorly stacked, and is then difficult to straighten. Birch ply should not be exposed to damp unless it is a WBP grade. The edges will clean up well if you use a plane, followed by abrasive paper. The 3 and 4 mm. thicknesses are very common materials for drawer bottoms.

Gaboon and West African ply. Lighter and weaker than birch, they have less tendency to twist. When resin-bonded they can be used satisfactorily outdoors. Commonly used in furniture-making, but the edge is difficult to finish. Cresta, one of the most popular branded makes, is available in different qualities for indoor and outdoor work (with proofing against insects), or with combinations of these qualities.

Beech ply. A very tough ply, which twists unless stored flat or held in position by rails when made up into furniture. Resin-impregnated varieties are stable and extremely hard.

Parana pine. Quite hard, and takes a good finish, but it will wind in a corkscrew action if it starts to move. Not usually waterproof, and rots easily.

Douglas fir. Most commonly used for facing concrete and, in the thin sheets, 6–9 mm. thick, mounted on battens as wall panelling. The grain darkens when it is exposed. End grain is rather coarse and not easy to finish.

Sizes and grades

Lengths and widths of plywood are still sometimes given in feet or inches, but thicknesses are in millimetres (mm.).

In the chart below, figures in light type indicate sizes not generally available at do-it-yourself shops; these may have to be ordered from a timber merchant's.

Corners of sheets are seldom undamaged—allow for losing some of the sheet in cleaning it up.

Thickness in mm.	Usual sheet sizes mm.	in.	Unusual sheet sizes mm.	in.	Notes
0·8					Birch—exterior WSP
1·2					
1·5	1220 × 1220	48 × 48			
2·0	1270 × 1270	50 × 50			
3	1270 × 1270	50 × 50	1525 × 3050	60 × 120	
	1525 × 1525	60 × 60	1830 × 1220	72 × 48	
			2440 × 1220	96 × 48	
4	As above plus		3050 × 1220	120 × 48	Marine ply available
	2440 × 1220	96 × 48			2440 × 1220 mm. mahogany
5	1295 × 1295	51 × 51	3050 × 1220	120 × 48	
	1550 × 1550	61 × 61	3050 × 1525	120 × 60	
	2440 × 1220	96 × 48			
6	1220 × 1220	48 × 48	2440 × 1525	96 × 60	Marine ply available
	1525 × 1525	60 × 60	3050 × 1525	120 × 60	
	2440 × 1220	96 × 48			
8	1525 × 1525	60 × 60	3050 × 1220	120 × 48	As above
	2440 × 1220	96 × 48			
9	1220 × 1220	48 × 48	2745 × 1525	108 × 60	1525 × 1525 mm.—birch
	1525 × 1525	60 × 60	3050 × 1525	120 × 60	2440 × 1220 mm.—mahogany
	2440 × 1220	96 × 48			2745 × 1525 mm. ⎱ Douglas 3050 × 1525 mm. ⎰ fir
					Marine ply available
12	1220 × 1220	48 × 48	3050 × 1220	120 × 48	Marine ply available
	1525 × 1525	60 × 60	3050 × 1525	120 × 60	Birch and mahogany available
	2440 × 1220	96 × 48			
15	1525 × 1525	60 × 60	2440 × 1525	96 × 60	Marine ply available
	2440 × 1220	96 × 48	3050 × 1525	120 × 60	
18	1525 × 1525	60 × 60 (1)	3600 × 1220	144 × 48	(1) Birch
	2440 × 1220	96 × 48 (2)	3600 × 1525	144 × 60	(2) Mahogany
	3050 × 1525	120 × 60 (3)			(3) Douglas fir
					1525 × 610 mm. floor panels available tongued and grooved
22	1220 × 1220	48 × 48	3050 × 1220	120 × 48	
	1525 × 1525	60 × 60			
	2440 × 1220	96 × 48			
25	2440 × 1220	96 × 48	1830 × 1220	72 × 48	Mahogany,
	1525 × 1525	60 × 60	2135 × 1220	84 × 48	Douglas fir
	3050 × 1220	120 × 48	2440 × 1525	96 × 60	and Gaboon

Grading
Ply is graded according to the quality of the outer veneers. A is the highest grade and denotes that the veneer is without blemish: B is sound, but with small knots and occasional markings: BB is usually a veneer which has had dead knots and other faults cut out and patched.

For example, A/A means that both sides are perfect, and B/BB (the most common grade) has one side sound but with small defects, and the other side patched.

Techniques for different jobs

Plywood can be mortised, dovetailed, mitred and worked similarly to solid wood in many ways. provided it is thick enough. Avoid using plywood for drawer sides— the edge of ply is made up of edge grain, glue and end grain, which vary in hardness and wear unevenly, thus tending to cut the runners rather than slide.

Sawing

Cut 0·8–2 mm. with a knife; for other thicknesses, use a fine-toothed saw—from 2–6 mm. a dovetail or small tenon saw, from 6–12 mm. a tenon saw; above that a panel saw. Always mark a cut line with a knife when cutting across the grain, and cut on both sides of the sheet to prevent any breakaway.

Pinning and screwing

Always drill pilot holes before screwing. Pins and screws do not hold as well in the edge of ply as they do in the face. When soft ply is being fixed with screws, there is a danger that the screw heads may sink too far into the veneer. Use screw cups to reduce this risk. The hold in birch ply is better than in Gaboon and Douglas fir.

Gluing

Always rough-up the surfaces of ply so that the glue will have something to grip. Use coarse glass-paper or a toothing plane.

Apply as much even pressure as possible while the glue is setting. For marine or outside work, use a waterproof adhesive. If you join sheets of ply, they will remain more stable if the joining faces have the same grain direction.

Jointing

Plywood over 9 mm. thick can be jointed as ordinary timber. Joint edge-to-edge by the loose-tongue method but do not bend the sheets after jointing.

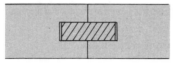

Leave gaps between tongue and groove bottoms

Repairing

If small pieces of laminated veneer lift during work, glue and cramp them in place again, using softening and paper.

Protection

Wherever possible, fix ply so that its edges are supported. Sharp blows to the edge often cause delamination and tearing. Protect the edges with lipping where there is a danger that they may be knocked.

Alternatively, remove the sharp edge with a small chamfer.

Bending

The thinner the sheet, the more it will bend. Birch is one of the best plys for bending.

Fairly simple, even curves will hold their shape if you bend two or more sheets of ply and glue them together, using temporary formers. Slight damping of what will be the outer curve of each sheet will help it to bend, but on no account glue the sheets together while they are still wet: let them dry out overnight in the new shape.

Ply will bend to a tighter curve when the grain is running across the curve than when it is running with it.

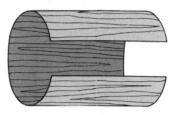

Ply bends more tightly like this . . .

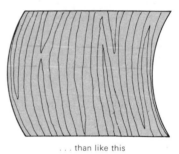

. . . than like this

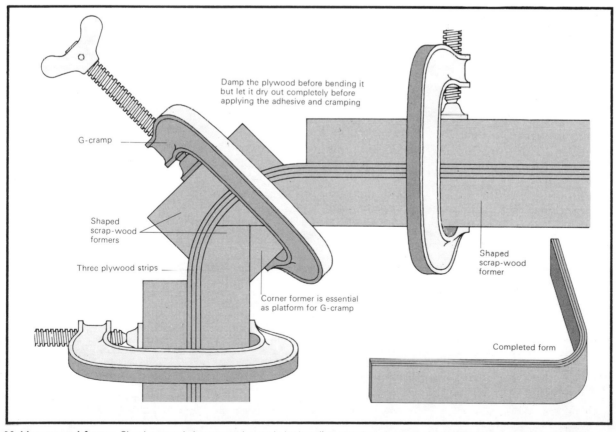

Damp the plywood before bending it but let it dry out completely before applying the adhesive and cramping

G-cramp

Shaped scrap-wood formers

Three plywood strips

Corner former is essential as platform for G-cramp

Shaped scrap-wood former

Completed form

Making curved forms. Simple curved shapes can be made by bonding together pieces of plywood between scrap-wood formers.

Woods/4

Hardboard

This versatile material is made from softwood pulp which is forced into sheets under high pressure. There are several types, although when most people mention hardboard they have only the standard varieties in mind.

Standard hardboard

This has a finished face on one side only and a rough mesh texture on the reverse. It is made in thicknesses ranging from 2 to 12 mm. The most common, 3, 4 and 6·5 mm., are fairly easy to obtain in sheets of 610 × 1220 mm., 1220 × 1220 mm., 1830 × 1220 mm. and 2440 × 1220 mm. and in 6 ft 6 in. × 2 ft 6 in. sheets for doors.

Most shops and timber merchants cut to size, but sometimes their cutting is inaccurate and out of square. Ask for a piece slightly oversize, so that you can trim it yourself. Ready-cut standard sheets are usually true and are up to 3 mm. bigger than the stated sizes.

Your requirements may make it cheaper to buy a crate containing 20 or more sheets.

Medium hardboard

This is a much softer board which is often used as a surfacing material for wall partitions. One of the best-known boards, Sundeala, makes an ideal notice-board because it takes drawing-pins easily.

Tempered hardboard

This board has been impregnated with oil to make it hard and water-resistant. It is useful for lining walls and ceilings in outbuildings. Another of its uses is as a finished flooring, over either boards or concrete. Thicknesses and sheet sizes are as for standard hardboard.

Double-faced hardboard

Each side of the sheet has a finished face. It is made in 2440 × 1220 mm. sheets and is available in cut sizes. It is generally available only in 3 mm. thickness although it is also made 2–12 mm. thick.

Perforated hardboard

The standard sheet sizes are 610 × 1220 mm., 1220 × 1220 mm., 1830 × 1220 mm. and 2440 × 1220 mm., usually 3 mm. thick but thicknesses of 4 and 6·5 mm. are made.

Except for pegboard, which is commonly single-faced standard hardboard, the sheets are usually double-faced. The perforations can be a simple series of holes or slats at regular spacings, or can form more complicated patterns.

Many of these sheets are oil-tempered.

Enamelled hardboard

This is frequently used for wall or bath panelling. It is standard hardboard with a factory-painted surface, often with tile or plank patterns embossed. Some of the paints are plastic-based and are extremely hard-wearing.

Plastic-laminate faced hardboard

These hardboards are faced, on one side only, with melamine or PVC. They are often used for sliding doors and are decorative and easily cleaned. They are not suitable for worktops or any surface which will be subjected to harsh treatment.

Moulded and embossed hardboards

These are mostly 3 mm. thick sheets with patterns embossed into one face. The patterns include reeds, woven texture, leathergrain, bamboo, tile patterns, grooves and linen-fold. All are obtainable to order.

Working with hardboard

When boards are delivered, store them flat and take care to protect the corners and edges from damage.

Normal woodworking tools are used for cutting, shaping and cleaning up the edges. Avoid damaging the surface; once the smooth top crust is broken, no amount of sandpapering will repair the damage.

The surfaces of all except the medium and plastic-coated hardboards have a ripple or hammer texture which shows up after painting. Nothing can hide this, but it will be less noticeable with matt or eggshell finishes, which are less reflective than gloss.

Conditioning

Where standard hardboard is to be used, the manufacturers recommend that you should condition the board to prevent possible buckling through a change in moisture content. This is especially important if using the board as an underlay to floor tiles etc.

To condition the board, lay it flat on the floor and scrub cold water into the back at the rate of 1 litre (2 pints) to every 2440 × 1220 mm. (8 × 4 ft) sheet. Leave the board flat on the floor for 48 hours to adjust itself to the moisture conditions in the house. Leave tempered hardboard for 72 hours.

Do not condition boards in this way if they are to be fixed in surroundings where there is continuous heating; instead, allow them to dry out to the level of the surroundings for 72 hours.

Cutting

Use a fine-toothed saw (a tenon saw is ideal), and always cut on the face side.

On pre-painted and plastic-covered boards, score the cutting line with a knife before sawing; this prevents the top skin from chipping.

To prevent any tear-away, support both ends of the sheet on the underside.

Take your time when sawing; do not force the saw, or it will either tear the sheet or jump out and score the surface.

Cleaning up

Planes, spokeshaves and abrasive papers all give a good finish to the edges of standard hardboards. On medium hardboards, use only abrasive papers.

Avoid damaging the top surface.

Gluing

All woodworking adhesives work well on untempered hardboard. If gluing to the face of the board, rough-up the surface of the board to give the adhesive a key.

Fittings

Always drive screws through hardboard, not into it.

When pinning, use hardboard pins which are specially designed with diamond-shaped heads to penetrate the tough skin and leave a neat indent which can easily be filled.

Panel pins tend to stand above the surface and are always evident through painted finishes.

Painting and papering

All hardboards except factory-finished ones must be primed with special hardboard primer or thinned emulsion paint.

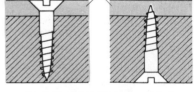

Screw through hardboard—not into it

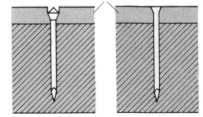

Hardboard pins leave small indents; panel pins remain visible

Use one part of water to four of paint.

Prime steel screws and pinheads before covering them with emulsion paint, otherwise they will rust and show through.

Seal hardboard with a coat of hardboard primer before hanging wallpaper on it.

Underlaying

Use sheets not larger than 1220 × 1220 mm. (4 × 4 ft) and stagger adjoining rows so that joints do not coincide. Fix hardboard to wooden floors with annular nails every 100 mm. (4 in.) at the edges and at 150 mm. (6 in.) spacings elsewhere. Lay the mesh side uppermost, to hide the nail heads, except when thin vinyl tiles are to be bonded to the hardboard.

Blockboard

Blockboard, like hardboard, is bonded under high pressure. The glues employed limit its use to inside work.

The most common blockboards are made from rectangular strips of softwood, bonded edge-to-edge to form a core which is sandwiched between single or double veneers of birch.

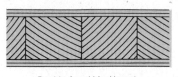

Single-faced blockboard

Double-faced blockboard

Blockboard veneered with West African mahogany is available in complete sheets from some timber merchants.

The most common sheet size is 2440 × 1220 mm., but others (1830 × 1220 mm., 2745 × 1220 mm. and 1305 × 1220 mm.) are available and cut sizes can usually be obtained.

The following sizes are less easily obtainable: 2440 × 1525 mm., 3050 × 1525 mm., 3660 × 1220 mm., 3660 × 1525 mm. and 4880 × 1525 mm.

Thicknesses are available at 12, 16, 19, 22, 24 and 32 mm. Also made, but not easily obtainable in some regions, are sheets 38, 44 and 50 mm. thick.

The core material runs the length of the sheet, making it stronger in its length than in its width. The grain of the veneers runs across the width. Single-faced boards have one veneer on each side, double-faced boards two.

Make sure, when using blockboard for table tops and large doors, that the core runs the length of the table top or from top to bottom of the door. The finished job will have less tendency to bow.

Movement. Blockboard can twist, bow, shrink or expand slightly, but careful attention to storage will reduce the risk of movement.

Shrinkage of more than 3 mm. in 1200 mm. ($\frac{1}{8}$ in. in 48 in.) is exceptional. Movement in the thickness is slight.

Shrinkage is more noticeable with the birch veneer than with the mahoganies. The birch also tends to 'check' into a series of fine lines. This checking is more of a problem with single-veneer boards, where the veneer is thicker, than with double veneers.

Storing. Never lean board against a wall. Lay it flat if you can; if space will not allow this, stand it on its edge as near to the vertical as possible. Do not lean anything against it.

Should the board become bowed or twisted, correct it by applying a load.

Covering. Painting one side of a sheet of blockboard creates surface tensions which pull it into a curve. By painting both sides, the surface tensions are equalised and the board keeps its original shape.

The same principle applies to papering, face veneering and polishing.

Edges. Lip all panels on exposed edges, as they are difficult to clean up to a good finish.

Use softwood lipping for painted work, matching hardwood for boards which have been faced with a decorative veneer.

Decorative veneers. Blockboard can be bought with a decorative face veneer which has been bonded on after the board has been made.

Face veneers are bonded so that the grain runs in the direction of the core: i.e. with the length of the sheet.

Unless specially ordered, face-veneered boards will have the selected face veneer on one side only. The reverse will be veneered in a cheaper timber, often one of

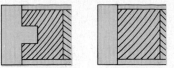

Tongued and butted lippings

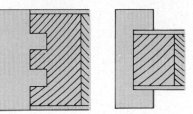

Double-tongued and moulded lippings

the cheaper mahoganies. Delivery of teak, oak and mahogany is usually quite prompt, if not from stock. But other veneers may have to be ordered and could take some weeks to arrive.

Laminboard

Laminboard has a core made from strips of softwood narrower than those used in blockboard. Otherwise, the two boards are constructed in the same way.

One of the advantages of laminboard over blockboard is in the surface finish of its face veneers. The core of blockboard often registers its pattern, seen as a regular ripple, through the veneers. This is known as 'telegraphing' and is not always visible until a high finish is put on the outer face. Double-veneer blockboards are less likely to telegraph, and the chance of this happening is reduced still further in the smaller core stock of laminboard.

Laminboard is not more than 9 mm. ($\frac{3}{8}$ in.) wide

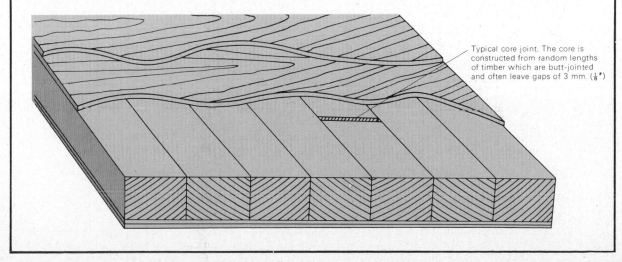

Cut-away detail of a double-faced sheet of blockboard. The veneer on single-faced boards is usually thicker than on double-faced.

Typical core joint. The core is constructed from random lengths of timber which are butt-jointed and often leave gaps of 3 mm. ($\frac{1}{8}$")

Woods/6

Chipboard

Chipboard is made by spreading resin-coated particles of wood, usually softwood, on a flat plate and bonding them together under high pressure and heat.

Thicknesses of chipboard vary from 4 to 40 mm., but the most common available are 12, 18, 22 and 24 mm. Sheets are usually 2440 × 1220 mm. (8 × 4 ft), but sizes up to 5200 × 1830 mm. (17 × 6 ft) are made. Both British-made and imported varieties are widely available in several grades of hardness.

The fibres of the particles criss-cross, so that the board has similar strength and characteristics in all lateral directions, but the vertical structure is layered.

Most chipboard is now made in three or more alternating layers of fine and coarse particles, with fine particles on the faces.

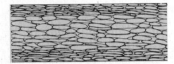

Three-layer: sandwiched chips

There is also single-layer chipboard, which tends to have a coarse surface finish because large chips are used.

Extruded: chips run from face to face

In extruded chipboard, which is now obsolete, the chips run from face to face and the board is easily snapped across its width. If you have any extruded chipboard, do not use it for furniture-making.

Modern multi-layer chipboards usually have sanded faces and some types are sealed and filled, ready for painting. There are also chipboards for special purposes, such as flooring, and veneered and melamine-faced chipboards.

Prices vary, but chipboard is generally half to two-thirds the price of blockboard.
Use: normal chipboard is for indoor use only and should not be used in damp conditions. Exterior-grade boards are not yet readily available.
Sawing and planing: use a panel, tenon, circular or jig saw. Finish the edges with a plane and glass-paper. Chipboard machines well, but wears cutters more quickly than softwood because of its resin.
Jointing: chipboard can be jointed in the same way as solid wood but with one exception—do not make unsupported edge-to-edge joints to increase the width of a panel: the layered structure makes joints of this type very weak.
Fixing: always pin, nail and screw through chipboard. Never pin, nail or screw into the edge; the fixings will pull out easily.

Where hinges and other fittings have to be screwed to chipboard, fit solid timber lippings for piano-hinges, butt-hinges etc., and dowels for single fittings with only a few screws. Hardwood dowels give the screws something solid to grip into and spread the load over a wide area.
Gluing: chipboard can be glued with any woodworking adhesive, but urea and thick PVA are best. The most effective bond is to the face. When gluing lipping to the

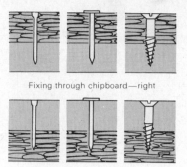

Fixing through chipboard—right

Fixing into chipboard—wrong

layered edge, use a tongued joint if possible, but a well-glued butt joint will do.
Storing: store sheets flat, but if space will not allow this, stand them on edge in a vertical position and secure them so that they do not become distorted.

Flaxboard

This material, commonly used in furniture-making as a core in veneered sheets, is lighter than chipboard but is just as stable and slightly cheaper.

It is becoming more readily available in thicknesses of 19, 22 and 25 mm.

In 22 and 25 mm. thicknesses, flaxboard is often used in its unsanded state as a decking material for mineral-felted roofs of garages etc., where it is nailed with large-headed galvanised clouts direct to the joists at 600 mm. (24 in.) spacings.

Flaxboard smells strongly of new-mown hay, unless completely sealed by veneer or paint, and the smell can be overpowering in a confined space.

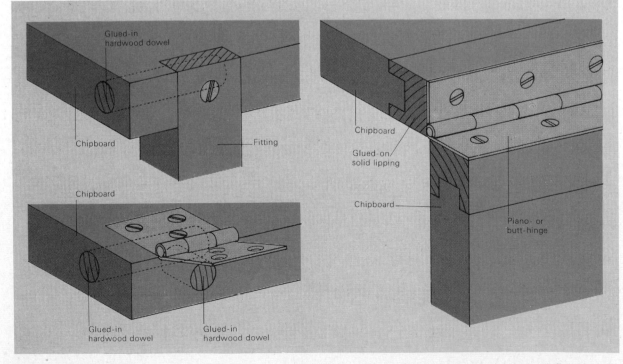

Insert hardwood dowels into chipboard to take screws for small fittings: edge the board with solid timber for larger fittings.

Building boards

The huge range of boards made for lining walls and ceilings are known as building boards. The term also covers the various types of hardboard and chipboard and many others not used in furniture making. These fall into three principal groups.

Insulating boards

These lightweight, porous boards, made from fibre, provide thermal and sound insulation. Their colours vary from cream to brown and grey, though some types are factory-finished with white paint.

Some insulating boards are impregnated with bitumen for greater water resistance and flame-retardant grades are also made.
Sizes: the usual width is 1220 mm. (4 ft), in lengths from 1830 to 3660 mm. (6 to 12 ft), but 610 mm. (2 ft) widths are also available. Thicknesses are 12, 18 and 25 mm.
Cutting: use a sharp trimming knife for a clean cut, or a fine-tooth tenon saw.
Fixing: nail insulating boards to studs with 40 mm. ($1\frac{1}{2}$ in.) galvanised clout nails spaced 100 mm. (4 in.) apart at edges and 200 mm. (8 in.) elsewhere. The stud centres should be no more than 400 mm. (16 in.) apart for 12 mm. boards, 600 mm. (24 in.) for thicker boards. Nail small areas so that they are fully enclosed.

Joints: cover joints with wooden fillets.

Advice on working with insulating boards, and with hardboard, is given by the Fibre Building Board Development Organisation Ltd., 6/7 Buckingham Street, London WC2N 6BZ.

Asbestos boards

A variety of asbestos boards, ranging from asbestos-cement to asbestos insulating boards, are made for use where fire-resisting qualities are necessary.
Sizes: 1220 and 610 mm. (4 and 2 ft) are the most common widths, with lengths ranging from 1220 to 3660 mm. (4 to 12 ft). Thicknesses range from 3 mm. for fully compressed asbestos-cement boards to 25 mm. or more for asbestos insulating boards.
Cutting: use a hacksaw or metal-cutting power saw for the hardest grades; a fine-toothed hand-saw can be used for asbestos insulating board grades. Trim edges with a file or Surform.
Fixing: drill holes and use galvanised clout nails or rustproof screws.
Joints: fill or cover joints, which can be tightly butted.

Follow the manufacturer's recommendations for decorating asbestos boards.

Plasterboard

Plasterboard consists of a core of plaster of Paris sandwiched between two sheets of heavy paper. Some plasterboards have aluminium foil backing to provide increased heat insulation.

Plasterboard can be used with the grey side outwards for skim-coating with board-finish plaster, or the ivory side for painting or papering. Before papering or painting plasterboard, seal it with a primer recommended by the manufacturer.
Sizes: eight lengths from 1830 to 3660 mm. (6 to 12 ft) are made in widths of 610, 915 and 1220 mm. (2, 3 and 4 ft). Thicknesses are 29 and 12 mm.
Cutting: use a fine-toothed saw or a trimming knife. Score the paper on one side with the knife, crack the board along the scored line and then cut the paper on the other side. Cut edges can be trimmed with a Surform (see p. 20).
Fixing: nail to studs with 40 mm. ($1\frac{1}{2}$ in.) galvanised clout nails at 150 mm. (6 in.) intervals. Cover the nail heads with filler.
Joints: leave 3 mm. ($\frac{1}{8}$ in.) gap between boards and fill the gap with special joint filler. Joints can also be covered with paper, cotton or linen sealing tape. Some tapes are self-adhesive.

Building a stud partition

Stud partitions are lightweight, non-load-bearing structures, usually faced with building board, which are used to divide buildings into rooms or to subdivide existing rooms.

Door openings, hatches or borrowed lights—interior windows which pass light coming from a window on an exterior wall—can be inserted in stud partitions.

Before you erect a partition in your house, always consult the local authority to make sure that the result will comply with constructional and public health standards.

The principal components of a stud partition are the vertical members, called studs, and two horizontal members—the head, fixed to the ceiling, and the plate, fixed to the floor.

The basic frame is completed by short horizontal pieces of timber, called noggings, fixed between the studs.

The simplest form of stud partition comprises a framework of 75 × 50 mm. (3 × 2 in.) timber covered on each side with 18 mm. ($\frac{3}{4}$ in.) insulating board. The joints in the insulating board are covered with wooden fillets and a skirting is fixed to the bottom of the partition to protect the boards.

The head must be fixed to the ceiling, so before you build a stud partition, check on the positions of the joists.

If the line of the proposed partition runs across the joists, it can be fixed anywhere. If it runs parallel to the joists, move the partition to come under a joist, or else fit bridging pieces of timber between the joists on each side of the partition. Access

to the joists can be gained by taking up floorboards in the room above.

With a bradawl, pierce the plaster along the line where you wish to build the partition until you find a joist. Pierce a few more holes to establish the centre of the joist, and mark its position.

Find the centre of the next joist, which may be either 400 or 460 mm. (16 or 18 in.) away. Then mark the centre of every second joist.

If you are building the partition along a joist, mark the position of the head on the ceiling. Then, using a plumb-line or spirit level, mark the walls. Finally mark the position of the plate on the floor.

If you are building across the ceiling joists, you can mark the plate position first, then mark the walls and the ceiling.

Cut the plate to length and mark out the positions of the studs, starting at one end. The studs are spaced at centres 610 mm. (2 ft) apart, to permit easy fixing of building boards, except at the ends of the partition, where an allowance has to be left for scribing the board to the wall.

Position the first stud at the end of the plate, the third with its centre 1210 mm. (3 ft $11\frac{1}{2}$ in.) along and the second centrally between them. This allows 10 mm. ($\frac{1}{2}$ in.) for scribing the board to the wall.

Position the rest of the studs at 610 mm. (2 ft) centres. Make allowance for scribing the last board to the wall if necessary, but the last two stud centres will probably be less than 610 mm. apart anyway.

Repeat the process for the head and then cut through-housings (see p. 38) for the studs in the plate and the head.

Drill 6·5 mm. ($\frac{1}{4}$ in.) dia. clearance holes for No. 12 screws through the plate every 610 mm. Lay the plate in position and mark where the holes come on the floor.

Drill holes for plugs in concrete floors, pilot holes for screws in timber.

Use 89 mm. ($3\frac{1}{2}$ in.) screws in a concrete floor, but 63 mm. ($2\frac{1}{2}$ in.) in a timber floor, so that there is no danger to pipes or cables beneath the floorboards.

Drill the head for screwing to the ceiling; nailing will dislodge plaster.

Screw the head and plate in position, and measure the lengths between the housings, using two pieces of batten.

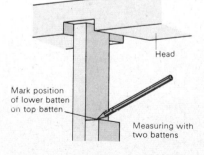

Mark position of lower batten on top batten

Head

Measuring with two battens

Cut the studs to length and fix them to the head and plate with skew-nails (see p. 170), taking care not to hit too hard. Alternatively, drill the studs and screw them to the horizontal members.

Skew-nail 75 × 38 mm. (3 × $1\frac{1}{2}$ in.) noggings to the studs, the centres 1220 mm. (4 ft) and, if the room is over 2440 mm. (8 ft) high, 2440 mm. above the floor.

Make a door opening by housing a

Woods/8

Building boards

75×50 mm. (3×2 in.) door head into two studs. Use a door lining wide enough to cover the edges of the insulating board and join the vertical and horizontal members of the lining with groove and rebate joints.

When the door is hung, check that it will swing without catching the floor, as the floor may not be level.

Make borrowed lights in the same way as door openings: house a 75 × 50 mm. sill into the studs and house central rails into the top and bottom linings.

Secure the glass between two glazing beads. It must be set in putty or it will rattle.

A hatch, with hinged or sliding door, can also be inserted into a partition. Line the opening like a borrowed light aperture.

Nail the insulating board only where the heads will be covered by the timber fillets.

Cut the first board about 10 mm. ($\frac{1}{2}$ in.) less than the room height and tack it lightly in position, touching the wall where the first stud was set out on the plate.

Scribe the board to the wall with the compasses set at 10 mm.

Cut the board to the scribed line and fix it to the partition.

Fix all boards tightly against the ceiling, leaving a 10 mm. gap at the bottom, where it will be covered by the skirting.

Fix the last board partition temporarily to the second last and scribe it 1220 mm. (4 ft) from the wall, keeping the marking rule level. Remove the board, cut it to the scribed line and fix it to the partition.

Fix a skirting-board—matching those elsewhere in the room—to the studs or plate with 50 mm. (2 in.) oval nails, and punch their heads below the surface.

Cover the joints with 50×12 mm. planed timber fillets. Fix fillets along the ceiling junction, then vertical fillets. Scribe the ceiling and wall fillets to the plaster.

Use 40 mm. (1½ in.) oval nails and punch their heads below the surface.

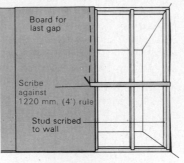

Scribing the last board

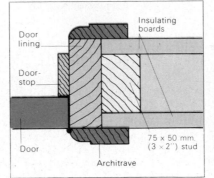

Detail of door-frame.

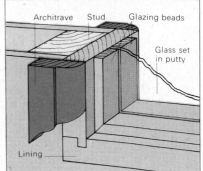

Detail of borrowed light.

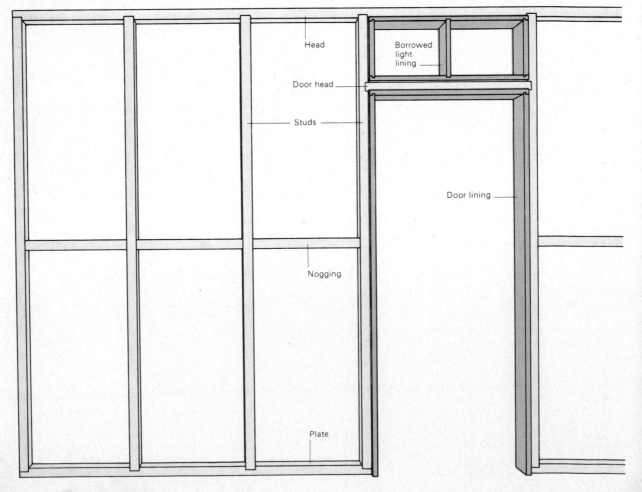

Points to watch when buying

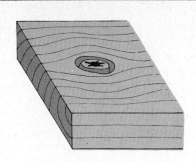

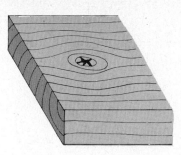

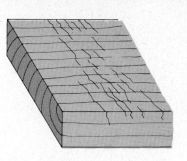

Dead knots have a black surrounding ring. Avoid such timber if possible, or cut out and patch.

Live knots, unless large, are acceptable in building. For furniture, avoid all but small knots.

Felling or compression shakes are areas of grain which have been distorted. Discard affected timber.

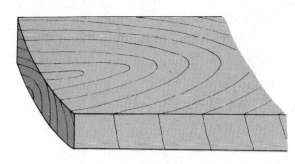

Warped boards. If the curl is across the width, rip into narrow strips, plane the edges to 90° and rub-joint together. If the curl is lengthways, cut into short lengths.

Cup shakes are caused by the centre or heart area of the tree drying out more quickly than the remainder of the timber. Cut out and discard the damaged area.

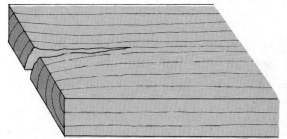

Waney edge, consisting of bark and sapwood, is often left on hardwoods. Both must be removed. The sapwood shows as a paler band of timber and is about 2 in. wide.

End shakes, due to faster drying at the ends of boards, are found in most lengths. Discard the affected part or saw along the grain, plane, and rub-joint together.

Dampness

If you use damp timber, you risk shrinkage, warping and glue failure as it dries out.

Wood from an open-sided store will contain up to 17 per cent of its weight in water—its moisture content. Under centrally heated conditions, this content will drop to about 8 per cent.

If you can, order kiln-dried timber which will be ready for use. Old, well-dried timber may not necessarily be a better buy than new—it often twists when re-sawn.

The best way to avoid the hazards of damp timber is to store it for at least three or four weeks in the room where it is to be used.

Keep a small stock of softwood for general use; buy hardwood well in advance and store it until you can do the work for which it is required.

To get a rough idea of whether a board is dry enough for use, saw through it about 230 mm. (9 in.) from the end. If the exposed end feels damp, further drying is needed.

For a more exact guide, cut a piece off a board (not the first 230 mm.), weigh it and leave it in a low-heat oven, checking the weight from time to time.

When the weight does not drop any more between tests, the wood has reached its dry weight, and the difference between the original weight and the dry weight is the lost weight.

Next work out the original moisture content of the wood as follows:

$$\frac{\text{Lost weight} \times 100}{\text{Dry weight}} = \begin{array}{l}\text{percentage moisture}\\\text{content of original}\\\text{sample}\end{array}$$

The satisfactory moisture content of wood for most indoor work is 10 per cent. If the content, as shown from the above formula, exceeds that percentage, it should be reduced accordingly.

Weigh the whole board, store it in a warm, dry place and check the weight frequently until the board is in a satisfactory condition for working.

Measuring/1

Squares, bevels and templates

The try-square is a vital tool, for marking out and checking right angles. Without one it is impossible to true up any edge.

The traditional try-square has a wooden or plastic stock and metal blade. A wooden-stock square may not always be true, since varying moisture content in the stock causes it to swell or contract.

To check a square for true, draw a line along the blade from a straight-edge, turn the blade over, and check that the blade coincides exactly with the drawn line.

The metal combination square will always stay accurate. It also has the advantage that it can be used for marking mitres (angles of 45°) as well as internal and external right angles.

Always hold the stock firmly against the work when using a square. Mark lines against it with a pencil or marking knife.

Marking knife

Other useful marking tools are the sliding bevel, which has a movable blade for marking and checking complex angles, and the dovetail template, which has sides with a 1-in-6 or 1-in-7 taper.

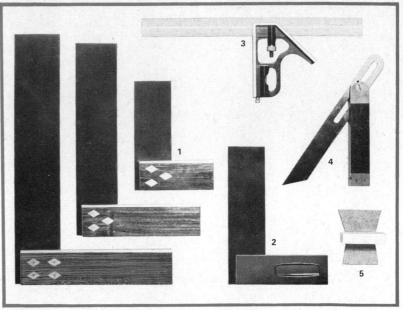

1. Wooden-stock squares can be obtained with blades 100–300 mm. (4–12 in.) long. **2.** The plastic-stock square stays accurate because there is no moisture movement in the stock. **3.** Combination square. **4.** Sliding bevel. **5.** Dovetail template.

Combination square. Hold the mitre edge of the stock against the work for marking or checking 45° angles. Make sure the locking nut is fully tightened.

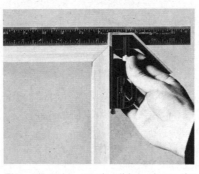

The adjustable stock slides along the graduated blade and locks anywhere on it with complete accuracy. Here the square is being used to check an outside angle.

Slide the blade right along for checking inside corners. The stock should overhang slightly, so that the corner of the blade can clear any small obstruction.

Gauges for marking and cutting

Gauges are for marking or cutting lines parallel to a face or edge.

The marking gauge is a necessary basic tool, for setting out for rebates and a variety of joints. To use it, you set the head the required distance from the pin, tighten up, then draw it along the edge so that the pin marks a line parallel to the edge.

The cutting gauge is similar to the marking gauge but with a cutting blade instead of the pointed pin. The blade is held in place by a wedge and must be kept sharp by honing. Use it to cut thin materials such as light plywood, cardboard and thin plastic, and to give a clear mark, particularly across the grain on wood.

The mortise gauge is a more elaborate version of the marking gauge which gives two parallel lines of varying distance. As its name implies, it is for marking out mortise and tenon joints: you set the two pins to the width of the chisel (which should

also be the width of the mortise) then set the head so that the pins will mark two lines, each the same distance from the edge of the wood. The width of a mortise should be about one-third of the width of the wood it is being cut in.

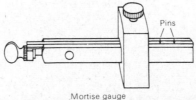

Mortise gauge

Handle all types of gauges the same way when using them: first push the gauge lightly along the wood, holding it firmly against the edge, then make a firmer, stronger stroke to give a clearer marking.

If the gauge tends to wander, pull it instead of pushing.

Grip the head of the gauge in the hand and always steady the wood which is to be marked against a bench-stop or similar support. Mark with the point or blade at an angle to the wood.

Rules, straight-edges and dividers

A 1 m./3 ft rule or 1 m./3 ft combination four-fold rule is the woodworker's basic tool. Metric graduations are in centimetres and millimetres, imperial in inches which are sub-divided into eighths and sixteenths. The more simple the rule, the better: types with protractor hinges and built-in spirit levels are of limited value and useless if a break occurs at the hinge.

A simple folding rule is best

Always use the same rule for measuring a space and for measuring up the wood to fit, as there may be some slight variation between rules.

Never use a dressmaker's tape for woodwork.

A little ingenuity will allow you to use a rule for jobs other than straightforward measuring. To divide a narrow board into six equal parts, for example, hold the rule at an angle across the board so that one end lines up with one edge of the board and the 6 in. mark with the other; make a mark where the figures 1 to 5 occur to give six equal divisions.

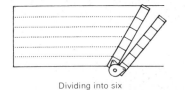

Dividing into six

Steel tapes of 2 m./6 ft and 3 m./10 ft have a loose lip at the end which hooks over the wood or butts up against it to assist accurate measuring. Longer steel tapes have a ring fixing at the end; these are not accurate enough for small work.

Steel straight-edges are made with or without measured graduations from 300 to 2000 mm. and 1 ft to 6 ft. Use these to check for flatness and as a guide for cutting against with a marking knife.

Checking a surface for level is done with a spirit level. The longer the level, the better check it will give over a wide area, though obviously a small level is better for confined spaces.

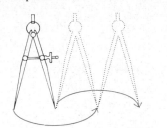

Use dividers with a swivelling action.

Dividers are useful for marking off a series of odd dimensions: simply set the dividers to the dimension on a rule, then mark out with the dividers at the constant setting. Dividers can also be used as compasses to mark a circle. They have the advantage over compasses in that they give a scratched line which is accurate, as, unlike the pencil point used in compasses,

the steel points do not become blunted.

To avoid a centre hole in the wood when using dividers, lightly glue a piece of thin metal or wood where the centre point of the dividers is to be placed and work from that, removing the padding piece immediately afterwards.

Apart from their obvious uses, compasses are used to mark a piece of wood for shaping to fit an uneven surface, such as a wall: hold the wood upright, about 10 mm. ($\frac{1}{2}$ in.) from the wall, then run the compasses down, the point on the wall, the pencil marking the wood to the exact contour of the wall. Keep the wood steady by putting packing pieces between it and the wall, and make sure that it is upright.

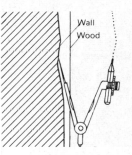

Scribing with a compass

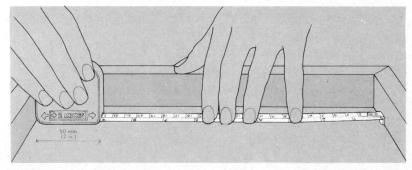

Inside measurements. When you are using a flexible steel rule, do not forget to add 50 mm. (2 in.) to the shown measurement, in order to allow for the case size.

Truing up wood step by step

The most vital operation in woodworking is measuring and marking out accurately. If this is inaccurate, the job is ruined from the start. Check work continually as you proceed, with rule, square and straight-edge.

No matter what shape a piece of wood is to end up as, it must have one flat face and one square edge to start with. All subsequent marking out is done from these two true surfaces; to achieve them follow this procedure.

First decide which of the two wider surfaces is the better, both in looks and grain. This will be your face side.

Plane this face until it is flat and level. Check across the grain with a steel rule for humps or hollows. Check any possible twist in the length, called 'winding', with two parallel battens (winding strips), one at each end of the timber. Sight across them and plane until they are level. Re-

member that the longer the plane, the truer the surface it produces.

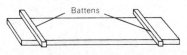

If battens are level so is the wood

Pencil a loop on the trued-up face with the end of the pencil line extending to the better of the two edges.

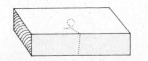

Marks for trued-up face and edge

Plane the face edge until it is straight and square with the face side. Check for square-

ness all along its length with a try-square. Hold the stock of the square firmly against the face side. If daylight shows between the wood and the blade at any point, the edge is not square and must be planed until it is.

When the face edge is true, continue your face side mark across the face edge. All subsequent marking out will be made from these two faces.

Now set your gauge to the required thickness and score a line from the face side along both edges. Plane carefully until you reach the centre of the gauge grooves. Then set the gauge to width. Mark both sides from the face edge, and again plane to the centre of the grooves. The timber is now squared up all round, ready for marking out.

To summarise: plane, test and mark the face side; plane, test and mark the face edge; gauge and plane to thickness; gauge and plane to width.

Measuring/3

Regular and irregular shapes

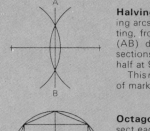

Halving a line at 90°: draw intersecting arcs, with the same compasses setting, from each end of the line. A line (AB) drawn between the two intersections will divide the original line in half at 90°.

This method is used in other examples of marking.

Hexagon: draw a circle with a radius equal to the side length required. Retain the compasses setting and step out the radius on the circumference of the circle six times (it works exactly). Connect the stepped-out points.

Octagon: mark out a square and bisect each side. Draw a circle, with the compasses point at the intersection of the bisecting lines (A), to enclose the square exactly. Draw lines joining the corners of the square to the points where the bisecting lines cut the circle.

Finding the centre of a circle: draw a chord (AB) within the circle. Use this as a base and, with a try-square, draw a rectangle within the circle. The intersection of the diagonals of the rectangle (C) is the centre of the circle.

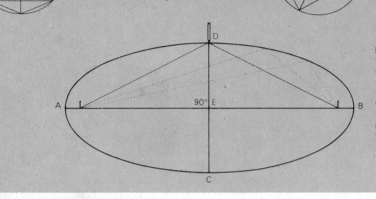

Ellipse: draw on centre line (AB) a bisecting line (CD) at 90°, so that they halve each other. Make the lines equal to the length and width of the ellipse. Set two pins along the centre line so that their distances from D equal half the length of AB (AE). Tie a loop of string that will go round the pins and reach the point D. Loop the string over the pins, insert a pencil and, keeping the string taut, draw the ellipse.

Drawing circles

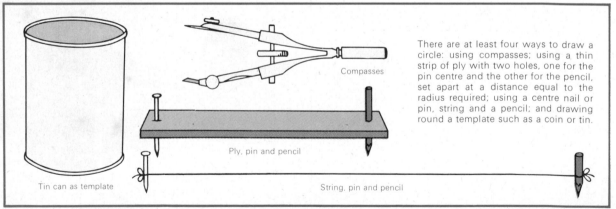

Compasses

Ply, pin and pencil

Tin can as template

String, pin and pencil

There are at least four ways to draw a circle: using compasses; using a thin strip of ply with two holes, one for the pin centre and the other for the pencil, set apart at a distance equal to the radius required; using a centre nail or pin, string and a pencil; and drawing round a template such as a coin or tin.

Curves

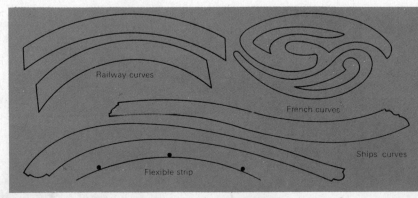

Railway curves

French curves

Ships curves

Flexible strip

Templates of radius curves, 38–6100 mm. (1½–240 in.) radius, can be ordered from a stationer, but they are fairly expensive. French curves, railway curves and ships' curves are available but are not usually stocked.

To get an even curve between three known points, use a thin wooden or steel strip. Hold the ends and flex it, so that it contacts all three points, and get someone to draw the curve.

Marking angles

1. Using a protractor or set-square. Once an angle has been found, it can be copied by transferring the setting to a sliding bevel.
2. Using a try-square for a 90° angle.
3. Marking a square with the sides equal to the width of the wood and drawing a diagonal to get 45°.
4. Using a single setting of the compasses to give angles of 60° or 120°. Draw a semi-circle from point A and mark off points on the semicircle. Join them to A.
5. Finding 45°, having marked the 90° angle with a try-square. Divide that angle with three swings of the compasses on the same setting from points A, B and C. Join point A with the intersection at point D.
6. Finding angles of 30°, 60° and 90°, using compasses with a single setting. Draw arcs from points A, B, C, D and E. Join up the intersections with point A.
7. Dividing an unknown angle into two equal parts with a single compasses setting. Draw arcs from points A, B and C. Join up the intersection at point D with A.

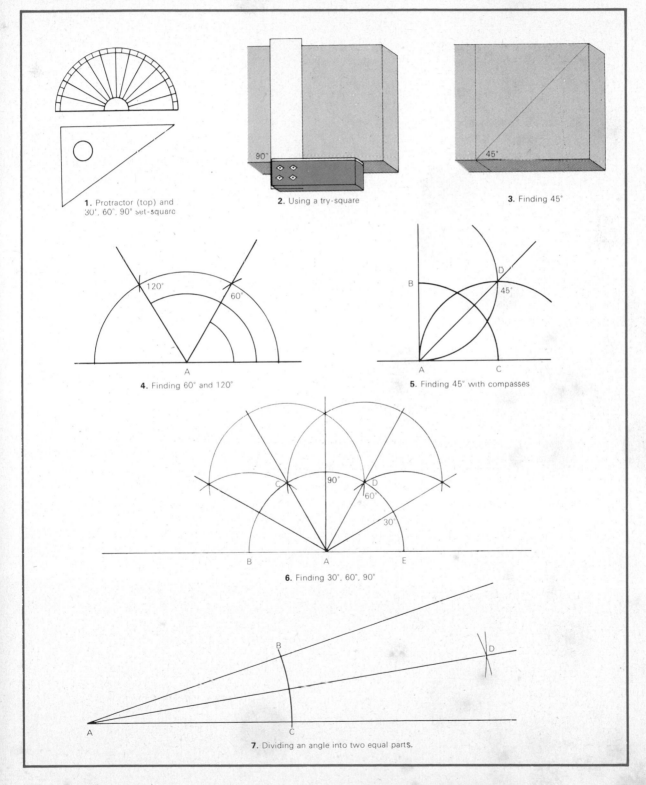

1. Protractor (top) and 30°, 60°, 90° set-square

2. Using a try-square

3. Finding 45°

4. Finding 60° and 120°

5. Finding 45° with compasses

6. Finding 30°, 60°, 90°

7. Dividing an angle into two equal parts.

Measuring/5

Corner curves

1. Use a coin as a template to mark a radiused corner on a piece of wood.
2. On a right angle, find the centre of arc by the 3-step method. With the compasses point in the corner, mark points A and C. From those points, with the same compasses setting, mark the intersection B, which is the arc's centre.

3. In acute angles, the centre of any circle contained within the sides is on the angle's bisecting line. Draw the curve with the compasses' point on that line.

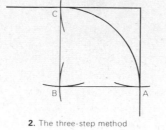

1. Using a coin

2. The three-step method

3. Finding the centre of an angle

Drawing a triangle

To form an equilateral triangle to fit a given piece of timber, find the centre of the shortest side, draw a semicircle to fit that side, and step off the radius once (D) from the lower corner. Draw a line between the top corner of the wood (A) and the stepped-off mark and carry it through to the bottom edge of the wood (B).

Set compasses to the length of the diagonal AB and scribe an arc, marking the wood at C. Draw a line from C to B.

To draw an equilateral triangle on a side of given length (AB), set compasses to that length, scribe the intersection C from A and B, and join up A, B and C.

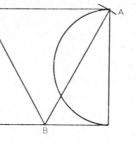

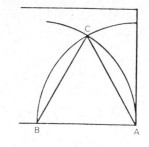

How to make a straight-edge

Bought straight-edges are usually of steel, but it is easy to make a wooden one from two pieces of 25 × 75 mm. (1 × 3 in.), 1200 mm. (4 ft) long planed, straight, even-grained timber.

Hold them together, face sides out and face edges together, with a pair of G-cramps. Run a long plane over the combined edges until continual, even, fine shavings appear. Uncramp and hold the two face edges together. Hold them up to a strong light. If light is seen through the joint, the edges are not true: re-planing must be carried out. Mark the gaps and plane the two edges together.

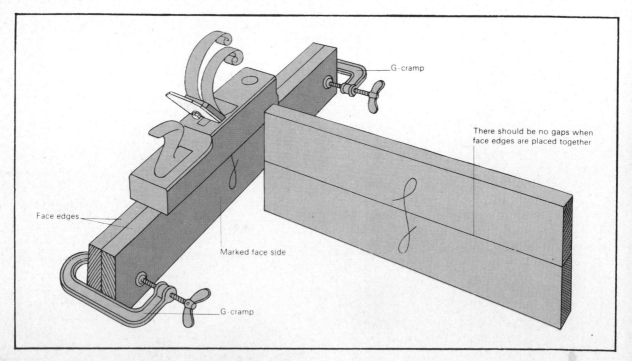

G-cramp

There should be no gaps when face edges are placed together

Face edges

Marked face side

G-cramp

Finding a vertical line

Plumb-bobs are machine-made, round-section weights which can be bought from most tool merchants. When tied to a builder's line or string and suspended from a pin or nail, a true vertical is struck by the line when the weight stops swinging.

By mounting the line and plumb-bob on to a board, the vertical line can be taken from the edge of the board with a pencil.

Make the board 100 × 25 mm. (4 × 1 in.) and 1500 or 1800 mm. (5 or 6 ft) long. Cut a hole [1] 12 mm. (½ in.) longer and 50 mm. (2 in.) wider than the bob [2] for it to swing in, and mark a centre line up the board [3]. Fix the pin into the centre line near the top of the board [4].

A bob can be made by hammering a piece of lead into an even shape.

When using a bob and board, make sure that the line swings free of the board.

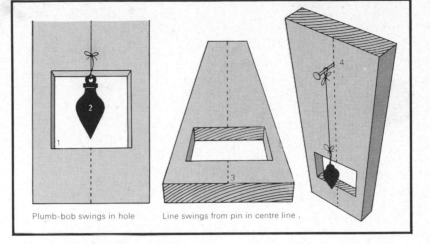

Plumb-bob swings in hole   Line swings from pin in centre line

Marking a horizontal without a spirit level

Make a thin ply pointer with a pin hole at the top and a point at the bottom, both exactly central to the edges of the ply. Firmly fix an upright board, wider than the pointer, to a straight-edge and draw a centre line through the board at 90° to the base of the straight-edge. Loosely pin the pointer to the board through the centre line, so that the pointer swings freely. Rest the straight-edge on top of the object to be levelled and move the object until the pointer lines up with the drawn centre line.

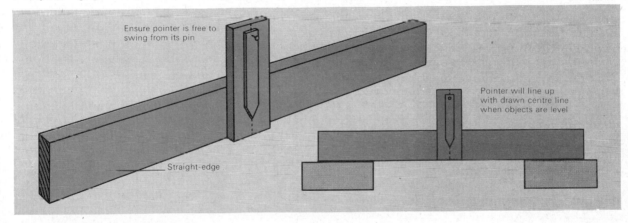

Ensure pointer is free to swing from its pin

Pointer will line up with drawn centre line when objects are level

Straight-edge

Checking levels

Fit a clear plastic tube into each end of a length of hose-pipe. Pour in water, ensuring that there are no air bubbles, until water shows in the plastic fittings. The water in the two fittings will be level—a useful guide for checking round a corner without a spirit level.

To check the level of a worktop or flat surface, stick a line of coloured tape along one side of a long glass dish, parallel to the bottom. Put water in the dish to a level just above the tape. Stand the dish on the surface to be checked. When the water level is exactly in line with the tape edge, the worktop surface is level.

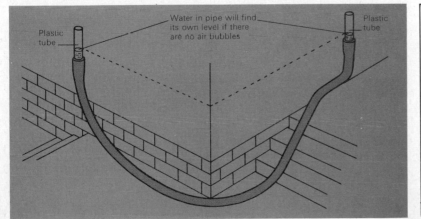

Plastic tube

Water in pipe will find its own level if there are no air bubbles

Plastic tube

Coloured tape is parallel to bottom of dish

Standing surface is level when water level is in line with tape strip

Joints/1

The joint for the job

To serve their purposes efficiently, wood joints must be marked out and cut accurately and put together with the correct adhesives and fastenings.

Difficulty in cutting accurately enough to make close-fitting joints can be overcome by using a sawing jig. With some jigs the angle of the saw is changed: with others the line of sawing is constant and the wood

itself is fixed at an angle to that line.

This section deals with the several variations of basic joints, from the simplest to the more difficult. T-joints, for example, start with simple nailed joints and finish with mortise and tenon and dovetail joints.

Joints can be divided into six groups:
T-joints: one piece is joined at right angles to the face or edge of another.

L-joints: two pieces form a corner.
X-joints: the pieces cross over or fix into each other to form a cross.
Edge-to-edge joints: edges are joined to produce wider surfaces.
Lengthening joints: two pieces are joined end-to-end.
Three-way joints: three pieces of wood are joined, e.g. a chair leg and rails.

Nailed T-joints

Simple nailed joints are quite good enough for light frames where the sides meet the cross-pieces flat on.

Cut the cross-pieces dead square, otherwise the joint cannot form a true right angle.

Drive the nails in from the outside whenever you can—this is easier than nailing from the inside. Use three nails: hammer the middle one in first to hold the wood

firm, then drive in the other two on either side of it, sloping them inwards at 20° to 30°. These nails form a dovetail which will lock the pieces of wood together.

Nailing from the inside of a frame needs more care because hammering tends to knock the cross-piece out of line. Prevent this by hammering from both sides alternately and re-aligning the work as the nail points begin to bite into the side piece.

Drive the nails in line with the grain, but stagger them a little to avoid splitting.

Punch the heads under for extra tightness. Fill the holes with stopping or putty before painting.

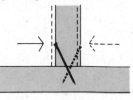

Take care the wood does not move as you hammer

Use oval wire-nails on wood up to 32 mm. (1¼ in.) thick, cut brads on thicker sections. The length should be at least twice the thickness of the side piece.

Nailed T-joints are only as strong as the nails that hold them together, but the strength and rigidity of a frame increases considerably if you cover it with hardboard or plywood.

Do not use nails on dry hardwood framing, as you may split the timber. Instead, make halving or tenoned joints which are described in this section.

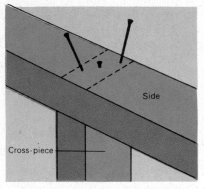

Nailing from outside. Slope the outer nails to form a dovetail for extra strength.

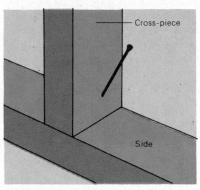

Nailing from inside. Hammer from both sides to prevent the cross-piece slipping.

Using brackets and fasteners

Metal brackets are a useful rough-and-ready aid to making flat T-joints. There are two types: one is a strip of drilled metal bent into a simple L-shape for fitting into corners; the other is in the shape of a T, and screws flat on to the work.

Use them whenever the appearance and thickness of the bracket do not matter, as in light framing which needs a little more strength than nailed joints provide.

Obviously, the stronger the bracket the

stronger the joint, but the brackets themselves will bend easily unless you use one on each side of the joint.

The screws should fit the drilled holes snugly. Drill pilot holes in the wood to prevent splitting. Drive the screws home flush with the bracket top.

A far quicker way to make T-joints is with corrugated metal fasteners which are hammered straight into the work. The fasteners are sharpened on one edge. They

are best used on light indoor work and in box-making.

Make sure that the joint is as tight as possible by putting the frame in a sash-cramp or pushing it against a fixed block before you drive the fasteners home.

Position the fasteners well in from the edges of the cross-piece to prevent splits. Tap the fasteners gently until they are going in evenly, then hit them centrally until they are flush with the surface.

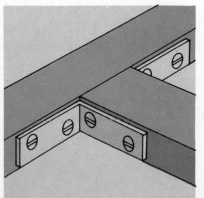

Two angle brackets help prevent bending.

A T-shaped bracket screwed flat.

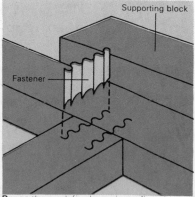

Press the work firmly against a fixed block.

Overlap joint

The overlap T-joint combines simplicity and strength for general-purpose jobs such as framing, fencing, shelving racks and lightweight gate construction.

It can be screwed, nailed or bolted and, for strongest results, should also be glued.

To make a screwed overlap joint, cramp both pieces of wood together with a G-cramp while drilling holes.

Drill a clearance hole through the top piece and a pilot hole in the lower piece with a twist bit small enough to allow the screw thread to bite firmly.

Countersink the holes in the top piece, coat both inner surfaces evenly with glue, fit the pieces together, and screw.

A simple glued and screwed T-joint, using supporting blocks, makes effective shelving units or bookcases.

Glue and screw blocks to each side of the casing, and then glue and screw the shelving to the blocks. On heavier shelving, —say, over 200 mm. (8 in.) wide—use the housing joint, described opposite.

A firmly fixed support block restricts shrinkage or expansion across the grain, which can be considerable.

Shelf-support blocks can also be screwed or masonry-nailed direct to the walls of alcoves.

To make a neat job, chamfer the exposed edges of the support blocks, or chamfer their front corners on the underside.

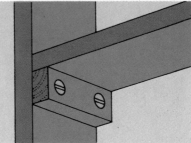

Overlap T-joint: position screws diagonally to avoid splitting the wood.

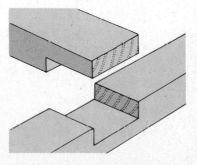

Support block: first screw the block to the upright, then screw in the shelves.

Full lap and half lap T-joints

These joints are far stronger and neater than the simple overlap construction. Use them for fitting cross-rails flush into frames which are to be covered in with panelling.

In a full lap joint the side rail is cut out to accommodate the whole of the cross-rail.

To make it, mark the exact shape of the cut-out on both faces of the side rail and across its top edge.

Cut out the waste with a tenon saw and chisel, paring away gradually from each side until the base of the cut-out is level.

Check the fit, glue all mating surfaces, and complete the joint by pinning or screwing.

In a half lap or T-halving joint, the cross-rail and the side rail are both cut away to give a flush fit when they are mated.

Mark the width of the cross-rail across the face of the side rail and half-way down both edges [1].

On the back of the cross-rail, mark a shoulder line across at a distance from the end a little greater than the width of the side rail.

Continue the line half-way across the edges. Set a gauge to half the thickness of the wood and gauge lines from the face of both pieces.

Saw a centre slot in the cross-rail, skimming the gauge line on the waste side [2]. Remove the waste block by cutting across the shoulder line.

Saw just inside the lines marking the side rail cut-out [3]. Saw an extra cut in the centre to make waste removal easier. Pare away the waste from both sides to complete the cut-out, check for fit [4], fix and trim.

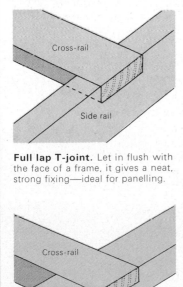

Full lap T-joint. Let in flush with the face of a frame, it gives a neat, strong fixing—ideal for panelling.

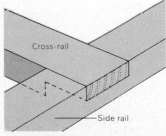

T-halving joint. A quick and simple method of jointing wood of equal thickness. Glue and pin the pieces together for greatest strength.

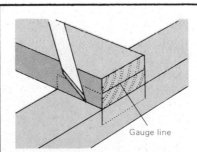

1. To make the T-halving joint, mark off the width of the cross-rail. Keep the pieces dead square to each other.

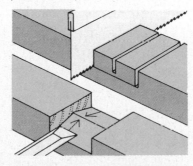

3. Make three tenon saw cuts—one on each side of the cut-out and one in the middle. Chisel the waste away from both sides down to the gauge lines.

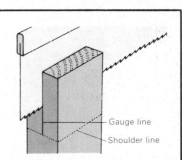

2. Saw down the centre of the cross-rail, cutting on the waste side of the gauge line.

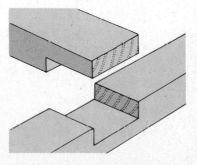

4. The finished joint should tap together easily. Make sure the shoulders are square. Glue and pin, allow the glue to set, then trim up.

Joints/3

Housing joints

The housing joint is the classic way of joining a board end-on to an upright. The housing, or cut-out, gives accuracy of assembly and great load-bearing strength.

There are two main types: the through-housing, in which the cut-out continues right across the upright, and the stopped housing, which neatly conceals its own construction on the front.

Both types can be dovetailed by cutting one side of the housing, and an end edge of the cross-member, at an inward-sloping angle.

The stopped housing is the better job for display and cabinet work.

Through-housing
To make a through-housing, mark a line square across the inner face of the upright, hold the cross-member against the line, and scribe another line against it to give the exact width of the housing [1].

Continue these lines square across both edges of the upright. Set a gauge to the depth of the housing—usually one-third of the upright's thickness—and gauge the depth line from the face side on both edges.

Cut down carefully to depth on both sides of the housing with a tenon or dovetail saw.

On long cuts, run the saw against a guiding batten clamped in place.

Chisel away the waste from each edge, beginning with gentle 30° cuts [2]. Gradually reduce the paring angle until the centre is chiselled away. Finish the cut with a hand router. If you do not have one, take extra care with the paring, and check frequently with a straight-edge for constant depth and flatness.

Cut the cross-member to length. Plane the end square, preferably on a shooting board, and fit the joint. After gluing and pinning, plane the front and back edges to a flush finish.

Stopped housing
The construction is similar to that of a through-housing except that the cut-out ends about 18 mm. ($\frac{3}{4}$ in.) from the front edge of the upright. The cross-member's front corner is cut away to overlap this.

Scribe the upright as for the through-housing, but leave the front edge un-marked. Mark the stopped end of the housing with a gauge from the front edge.

You cannot saw to depth unless you clear away a space for the front of the saw to move in, so chisel out 40–50 mm. ($1\frac{1}{2}$– 2 in.) from the stopped end to near the correct depth [3]. Then saw to depth from the back edge on both sides, again using a saw guide on longer work [4].

Chisel away the waste [5] and clean out to depth with a router.

On the cross-member, mark the cut-out to the depth of the housing and the length of the overlap. Saw away the waste with a tenon saw [6]. There is no need for the cut-out if the cross-member is designed to be set back from the front of the upright— just butt it against the end of the housing.

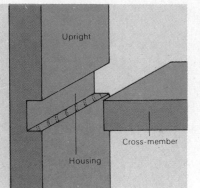
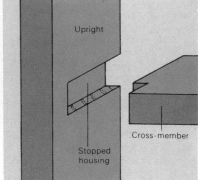

Through-housing joint. A clean, strong joint. The cross-member takes consider-able weight and is ideal for bookshelves.

Stopped housing joint. Use it where appearance matters. The overlap conceals the cut-out.

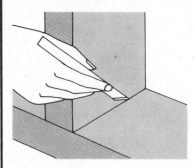
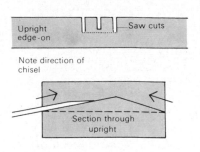

1. Place the cross-member against a squared line on the inner face of the upright, and scribe another line to give the exact width of the housing.

2. After sawing to depth, chisel out the waste gradually from each edge until the centre is removed. Trim to depth with a hand router.

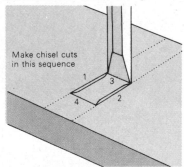
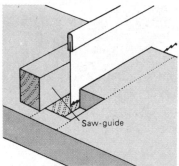

3. Make room for movement of the saw by chiselling a recess at the stopped end of the housing.

4. On long cuts, run the saw against a guide batten, temporarily clamped to the work with a bench holdfast.

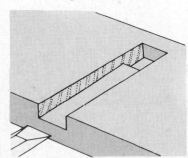
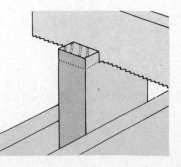

5. Chisel out the waste. Finish the cut with a hand router.

6. Saw off the cut-away on the cross-member to the depth of the housing.

Through mortise and tenon joint

This is the strongest of the T-joints. Use it on heavy framing and in general furniture work.

The thickness of the tenon, which is cut on the rail, should not exceed one-third of the thickness of the upright or stile.

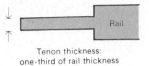

Tenon thickness:
one-third of rail thickness

To make the joint, mark the width of the rail on the stile, and continue the lines all round the stile.

On the outer edge of the stile, mark lines for the wedges—about 3 mm. (⅛ in.) outside existing lines. Then square a shoulder line right round the rail to give a tenon length just greater than the stile width.

Select your chisel—a mortise chisel is best, but a firmer chisel will do—and set the mortise gauge points to its width [1]. Centre the points on the edge of the work and mark off the mortise and tenon [2].

Cut the mortise [3], using either of the

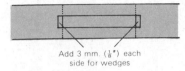

Add 3 mm. (⅛") each
side for wedges

methods described on p. 19. Then cut back to the wedge on the outer edge.

Saw down the tenon faces and cut carefully across at the shoulder lines [4–6].

Glue, assemble and cramp up, then hammer in the wedges [7–9]. Smooth off the protruding tenon end and wedges when the glue has set.

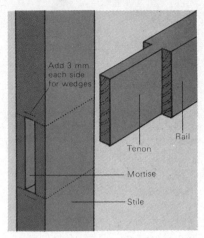

Add 3 mm.
each side
for wedges

Tenon

Rail

Mortise

Stile

Marking out: make the tenon long enough to project beyond the stile.

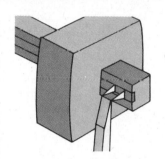

1. Set the points of the mortise gauge so that they just span the width of the chisel's cutting edge.

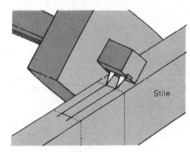

2. Centre the points on the edge of the work and mark both mortise and tenon from the face side.

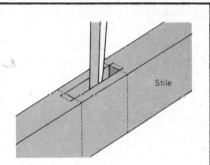

Stile

3. Chop out the mortise, working from both sides until the waste drops clear. Trim out, then cut back for the wedges.

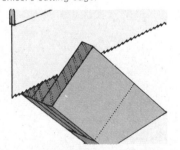

4. Make sloping cuts down both tenon lines from each edge alternately. Skim the lines on the waste side.

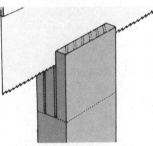

5. Clamp the rail upright in the vice, then saw the waste down squarely to the shoulder lines.

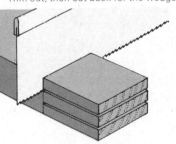

6. Cut across the shoulder lines to complete the tenon, making sure the saw is upright. Fit the tenon into the mortise.

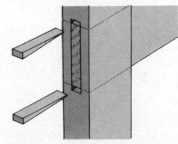

7. Apply adhesive to the tenon and inside the mortise. Fit the stile and rail together. Cut finely tapered wedges to fit part way into the 3 mm. (⅛ in.) slots at the ends of the mortise.

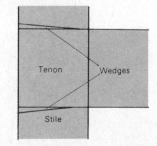

Tenon   Wedges

Stile

8. Apply adhesive to the wedges and drive them into the slots. Hammer both in at the same time, striking them alternately to keep the tenon straight in the mortise. Cramp the assembly.

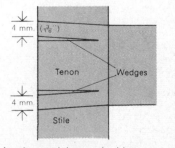

4 mm. (³⁄₁₆")

Tenon   Wedges

4 mm.

Stile

9. Another wedging method is to saw wedge slots about two-thirds down the length of the tenon, 4 mm. (³⁄₁₆ in.) in from the edges. The wedges jam the tenon into the shape of the mortise.

Joints/5

Mortise and tenon variations

Variations of the mortise and tenon serve two main purposes: to strengthen the joint for a specific job, and to hide the construction.

The commonest variation is to cut extra shoulders, reducing the width of the tenon by 3–12 mm. ($\frac{1}{8}$–$\frac{1}{2}$ in.) top and bottom.

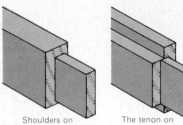

Shoulders on all sides

The tenon on double rebate work

These shoulders completely hide the ends of the mortise slot and the tenon itself. Check with a try-square and trim with a shoulder plane for a perfect fit.

On double rebated work, like the central rail of a frame intended for panelling, cut the tenon back to the width of the rebate on each side.

Both these variations are glued and wedged as described on the opposite page, or dowelled as described below.

Haunched tenon

This is the strongest possible joint for window-frames, doors and furniture. It can be used as an L-joint—on corners—as well as a T-joint. The haunch can be sloping, instead of square as shown below.

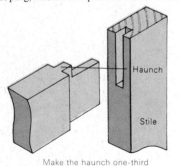

Make the haunch one-third the length of the tenon

The haunch resists twisting but does not over-weaken the stile, which the tenon would do if it were full width.

Proportions are important. Make the mortise and tenon about one-third the thickness of the wood—any wider, and the stile will be weakened.

Make the length of the haunch not more than one-third the length of the tenon. Its depth should be no more than a quarter of the width of the stile, or 12 mm. ($\frac{1}{2}$ in.)—whichever is the smaller. Often the depth is determined by a groove in the frame.

Leave at least 12 mm. waste on the end of the stile, to prevent splitting during the making and fitting of the joint.

The waste should remain uncut for as long as possible after the glue has set. It protects the corner until final fitting.

Double tenon

Use a double tenon where a single tenon would be so wide that it would weaken the upright.

The joint has great resistance to twisting where extra-wide rails have to be fitted to uprights. Set it out and cut it as for the single tenon.

The number of tenons need not be limited to two. Use any number, equally spaced, on very wide work such as carcase construction.

Multiple tenons, neatly wedged and trimmed, give a satisfying appearance on functional designs. Use power tools wherever possible because of the amount of tenon-cutting involved.

Stub tenon

This joint serves much the same purpose as the plain mortise and tenon, but the tenon is stopped short so that it does not appear on the outside.

Use it where appearances count, or where the full strength of the through-tenon is not needed, as in fixing intermediate rails in doors and carcases.

The depth of the mortise should be about two-thirds the width of the wood. Cut the tenon about 3 mm. ($\frac{1}{8}$ in.) short of this measurement to prevent it touching the bottom of the mortise.

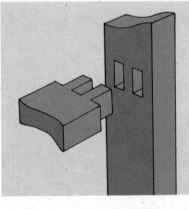

Double tenon. Make the widths of the tenons and the dividing gap the same.

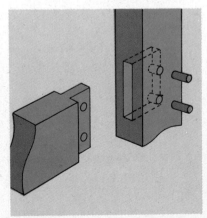

Stub tenon. The offset holes permit the dowels to jam the tenon in the mortise.

Use dowels through the stile and the tenon to give extra strength to the joint.

Scribed tenon

The scribed tenon is used where the work has one or both edges moulded, such as on window-frames.

Mark and cut both shoulders of the tenon to the depth of the rebate. Then, with a scribing chisel, cut away a concave shape in one of the shoulders to match the moulding on the upright.

An alternative and slightly simpler method is mitring. Cut mitres on each moulding on the rail and a corresponding recess in the moulding on the stile.

Twin mortise and tenon

This joint is mainly used on the centre rail, or lock rail, of door-frames. The divided tenons span the lock, which is mortised in from the outside.

The gap between the tenons is at least 38 mm. ($1\frac{1}{2}$ in.) wider than the lock so that the lock mortise will not seriously weaken the construction. There is a 12 mm. deep haunch between the two tenons to give extra resistance against twisting.

The joint should be used on any rail wider than 150 mm. (6 in.), even if no lock mortise is cut. A mortise the full width of the rail would seriously weaken the stile.

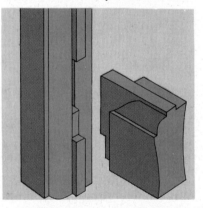

Scribed tenon. This joint is useful when repairing sash window-frames.

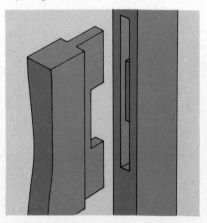

Twin mortise and tenon. The usual joint for centre rails of panelled doors.

Single dovetail

The single dovetail is a mechanically strong joint for rails which have to take weight.

To make one, mark out and cut the pin on the rail with a dovetail saw [1]. Make the slope of the pin 1 in 6 for softwood, and 1 in 8 for hardwood. Mark the shape of the pin all round the rail end and cut accurately to all lines.

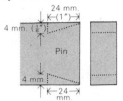

Typical measurements for dovetail—keep it as wide as possible

Transfer the pin shape to the frame piece [2] by marking with a pencil or knife.

Saw down the shoulders of the dovetail cut-out and make an extra cut in the centre of the waste to help chiselling out [3]. Tap the joint together dry before gluing, to check for fit [4].

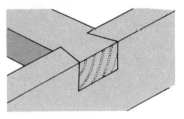

Trim pin when the glue has dried

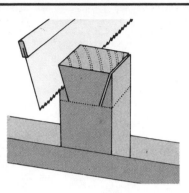

1. Cut the pin accurately to shape with the dovetail saw, skimming the lines on the waste side.

2. Mark the exact shape of the dovetail cut-out by using the pin as a guide for the pencil.

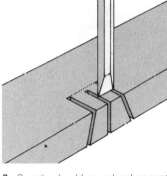

3. Saw the shoulders and make a centre cut to aid waste removal. Trim gradually to depth with a bevel-edge chisel.

4. Pare all shoulders and faces square so that the joint is a firm tap-fit. Glue after checking; trim when dry.

L-joints—six ways to make corners

Avoid elaborate joining of projects which are to be painted or where the appearance of the construction does not matter.

Modern glues, with screwing or dowelling, make strong corner joints. Six methods are shown on the right. The top three rely on corner blocks and the bottom three on metal or wood corner brackets.

The wooden corner blocks can be square or triangular in cross-section. The triangular shape [1] gives a neater appearance on the inside of cupboards.

The strength of these joints relies mainly on the glue; in addition to being glued, they should be nailed, dowelled or screwed together.

Hammer nails home dovetail-fashion (see p. 36). Stagger dowel or screw holes to avoid splitting the cross-piece along the grain. Make sure the dowels or screws do not meet in the middle.

Metal brackets can either be let into the top and bottom of the corner [4] or screwed straight on to the inside of the joint [5]. The first method is the stronger.

Metal brackets must be painted to prevent rust.

Triangular plywood brackets [6], also fitted top and bottom, are glued and pinned to the corner. Trim the outside edges when the glue has dried.

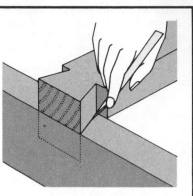

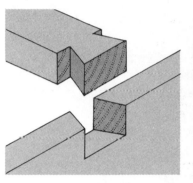

Triangular batten

Staggered screws

Outside batten

1. Use triangular blocks to get neat inside corners.

2. Square blocks give greater depth for screwing or dowelling.

3. Blocks can also be positioned on the outside.

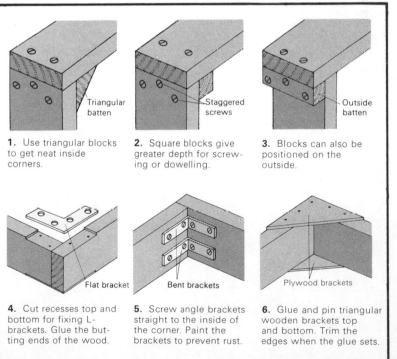

Flat bracket

Bent brackets

Plywood brackets

4. Cut recesses top and bottom for fixing L-brackets. Glue the butting ends of the wood.

5. Screw angle brackets straight to the inside of the corner. Paint the brackets to prevent rust.

6. Glue and pin triangular wooden brackets top and bottom. Trim the edges when the glue sets.

Joints/7

Rebated and grooved joints

Simplify drawer construction and other projects normally needing dovetailed corners by substituting rebated or grooved joints. They are quick to make and quite strong enough for most jobs.

Allow a little extra length on the front so that you can make the rebate slightly wider than the thickness of the wood it joins. This allows for final cleaning up. The depth of the rebate should be not more than three-quarters the thickness of the wood.

Cut the rebate with a tenon saw or on a bench-mounted power-tool attachment. Square up the end of the joining piece on the shooting board.

Glue and pin the joint, tapping the pins home in a dovetail formation for extra strength.

Use this joint on the front corners of drawers with the rebate overlapping the sides. The overlap will cover the grooves ploughed in the sides of the drawer to take the plywood drawer bottom.

For drawer fronts which extend beyond the sides, use a groove and rebate joint.

Cut the groove—a through-housing—in the inner face of the drawer front and the rebate on the inner face of the side. Both groove and rebate can be dovetail shape to give extra strength if required.

A shoulder plane is ideal for trimming both these joints.

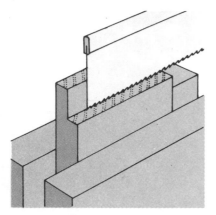

Sawing the rebate

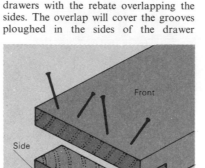

Rebated joint: when gluing, tap home nails in a dovetail shape for extra strength.

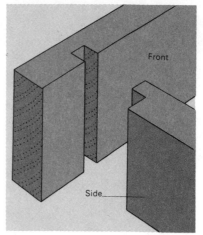

Groove and rebate joint: a good joint for an overhanging end.

Bridle joints and box joints

The bridle or finger joint is strong but needs to be well made to give a pleasing effect. It is ideal for jobs such as joining legs to chair arms.

Use the bridle joint at a corner [1]—where it is virtually a tenon running into an open-ended mortise—or at a T-joining [2] where it is stronger and more decorative than a plain halving.

For both types, set the points of a mortise gauge to divide the edge of the work into three. Square off the shoulder lines on both pieces and gauge in the finger and cut-out lines from the face sides. An ordinary marking gauge will do if you use two settings.

Mark the waste wood clearly with chalk so that there will be no sawing mistakes.

Saw down the cut-out section, skimming the gauge lines in the waste.

Remove most of the waste by cutting across near the bottom with a coping saw.

Square off at the shoulder line with a narrow chisel.

Cut the finger of a corner joint as you would a tenon. On the through-joint, produce the finger by using the halving cut-out method on both sides—sawing down to the gauge marks and chiselling out the waste from both sides.

Both joints can be further strengthened by dowelling through from the face side.

To get extra tightness, offset the dowel holes slightly so that the dowel, when driven home, forces the finger against the bottom of the cut-out.

The box or comb joint [3] is usually machine-made, but it can be made by hand as an alternative to dovetailing on light furniture and in box construction.

The setting out needs care: one of the meeting pieces must contain both end fingers; its total number of fingers will therefore be uneven.

Mark out with a mortise gauge, working from the same edge. Score each shoulder line with a marking knife. Rub chalk in to make the lines clearer and mark off the waste.

Check one piece against the other before you cut the joint.

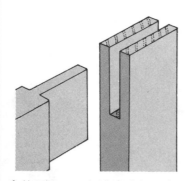

1. Use the corner bridle for jobs such as joining legs to chair arms.

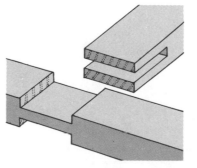

2. The through bridle gives a better finish than the plain halving joint.

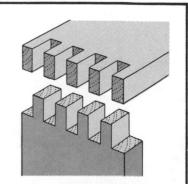

3. The box joint has many uses in the construction of light furniture.

Mitre joints

Mitre joints are used for picture-frames and larger jobs such as bookcases. The mitre angle of 45° must be cut and trimmed accurately for success [1 and 2]. It must also be strengthened in one of several ways.

The simplest strengthening method is gluing and pinning [3]. Glue both surfaces, then clamp the corner firmly in a vice between padding. This stops the pin hammer from knocking the joint out of shape. Tap the pins home in a dovetail shape and fill the holes.

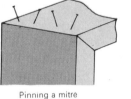

Pinning a mitre

A stronger method is to saw slots dovetail-fashion across the outer edge of the corner, with both pieces held together in the vice. Insert pieces of veneer or 1·5 mm. ply, and trim when the glue dries [4].

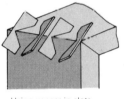

Using veneer in slots

Loose-tongue mitres are stronger still. Avoid damaging the edge of the mitre by making a 45° block the same width as the work [5]. Clamp the block and the work together in a vice and plough the groove, using the block as a guide. Cut the tongue from short-grain ply.

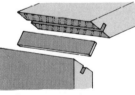

Loose-tongue mitre

Dowelling is also effective, but the holes need careful drilling. Locate them exactly by tapping pins at the dowel positions in one mitre face [6]. Snip the pins off and press them into the other face. Remove the pins and drill both sets of holes at right angles to the mitre.

Set the holes nearer the inner face of the work to allow a reasonable length of dowel.

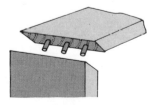

Dowelled mitre

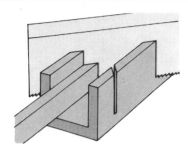

1. Cut the mitre carefully in a mitre box using a tenon saw. Make sure the moulding is the right way round.

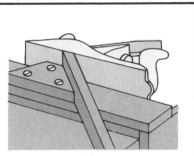

2. Trimming with a plane shortens the work a little, so allow about 1 mm. ($\frac{1}{32}$ in.) when sawing the mitre. Trim back to the exact length with a plane on a mitre board. Make sure the plane is sharp and give it a fine setting.

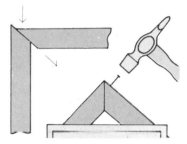

3. Pin a mitred corner with the joint held firmly in the vice to prevent the hammer from knocking it out of line.

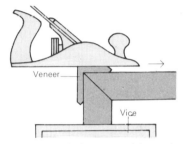

4. Plane towards the centre of the work when trimming ply or veneer let into corners dovetail-fashion.

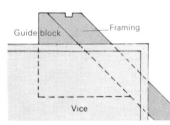

5. Use a 45° block the same width as the work as a guide for the plough plane in cutting a groove for a tongue across a mitre.

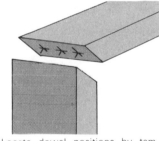

6. Locate dowel positions by temporarily tapping pins into one face. Snip them off short and make their impressions on the other face. Remove the pins, and the exact positions for all the dowels are marked. Use a depth gauge on the bit when drilling the dowel holes.

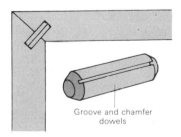

7. Dowels should have a groove sawn along them, to allow glue to escape. Chamfer the ends so that they will fit into the holes easily. Dip the dowels in the glue pot.

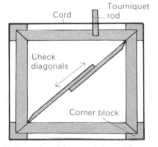

8. Pull a mitred frame tight with a cord running round corner brackets and tightened with a tourniquet rod. On all frames, check that the diagonals are equal.

Joints/9

Through-dovetail joint

The through-dovetail is the strongest and most decorative of the corner joints; it is used extensively for the backs of drawers.

Before you start, assemble all the pieces of wood to be joined and mark the mating pieces forming the corners, to avoid any mix-up later on. Then plane the ends of each piece on a shooting-board, allowing about 1·5 mm. ($\frac{1}{16}$ in.) for overall wastage.

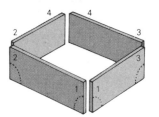

Mark all corners

Set the cutting gauge to the thickness of the wood plus 0·75 mm. ($\frac{1}{32}$ in.)—the allowance for waste on each corner. Mark gauge line (a) on all sides and edges.

The size and number of tails depends on the job. On a 100 mm. (4 in.) deep drawer, for instance, three 25 mm. (1 in.) tails will be ideal. On larger work, use coarser tails.

Use a dovetail template (angles 1:6 for softwoods; 1:8 for hardwoods) to mark the tails. Square the lines across the ends.

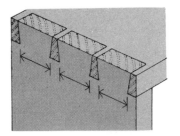

Space pins evenly

Cut down the tails with a dovetail saw, skimming the lines on the waste side [1]. Remove most of the waste with a coping saw [2]. Trim out with a narrow, bevel-edge chisel [3].

To mark out the pins, chalk the end grain and clamp the piece upright in the vice [4]. Place the tails over the chalked end, using a support block at the other end of the tail member. Then mark off the tops of the pins with a fine scriber, a needle or the tip of the dovetail saw. The lines will show up in the chalk. Continue them in pencil, square down to the shoulder line (a).

Cut down the pins with the dovetail saw [5], saw out the bulk of the waste with a coping saw and trim to the shoulder lines with the largest possible chisel.

Save time when making several joints by cutting all the tails at once with the tail pieces clamped together in the vice.

Test the joints for fit [6], leaving them dry at this stage in case further trimming is needed. If all is well, glue and cramp the carcase together. Finally, clean up the joints with a plane.

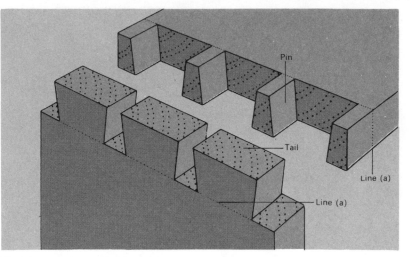

Marking out dovetails: the tails give greatest strength when positioned at the sides of drawers, carcases or upright frames.

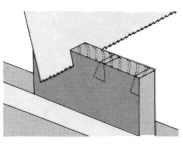

1. Cut the tails in the vice with a dovetail saw. Saw within the waste.

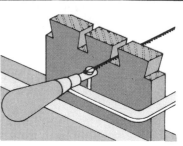

2. Remove the bulk of the waste with the coping saw. Take care not to saw into the tails. Hold the saw dead level.

3. Trim out the tails with a narrow bevel-edge chisel. Keep the work steady by cramping it with a bench holdfast.

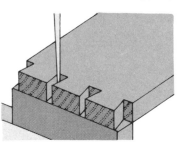

4. Mark out the pins by using the tails as a template. Use a fine scriber.

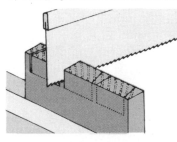

5. Saw down the pin lines, then remove the waste with a coping saw. Trim out with the largest possible chisel.

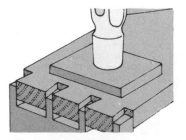

6. The completed joint should fit firmly when tapped together. Use a spare block to prevent the hammer damaging the surface. Position the pins at the top and bottom on frames, at the back on drawers.

Lapped dovetail

The lapped dovetail is used where the ends of the tails would spoil the appearance of the work, such as on drawer fronts, bookcases and better-quality framing.

The pins go on the lapping piece and the tails on the side piece.

Cut and plane the side to the exact length of the drawer, less the thickness of the lap—3 mm. ($\frac{1}{8}$ in.) on 19 mm. ($\frac{3}{4}$ in.) wood, a proportion of 1 : 6. Cut and plane the front to the size of the opening it has to fit.

Set the cutting gauge to the thickness of the front, less 3 mm. for the lap. Gauge line (a) on the end of the front and on the inside,

and line (b) all round the end of the side with the cutting gauge at the same setting. Mark the tails as for the common dovetail and cut them in the same way.

Butt the tails against line (a) on the front and mark off the shape of the pins.

Now mark the depth of the pins on the inside of the front. Saw the pins at 45°, with the wood held upright in the vice. Chop out the waste, keeping the chisel short of line (a) until the bulk is removed.

The overhang of the pins prevents cutting straight into their corners. Ease out the waste at these points.

Trim the inner faces of the pins by paring

with a bevel-edge chisel. Finally, run a groove for the drawer bottom through a tail so that it will be covered by the lap.

On bookcases or sideboard carcases, cut mitres between sides and the top and bottom on the corners that show.

Variations on the joint are the double lapped dovetail, which leaves only a small amount of end grain showing, and the secret, or mitre, dovetail which conceals its construction entirely.

In both the double lapped and the mitre dovetail joints cut the pins first.

Considerable experience is required to make these joints successfully.

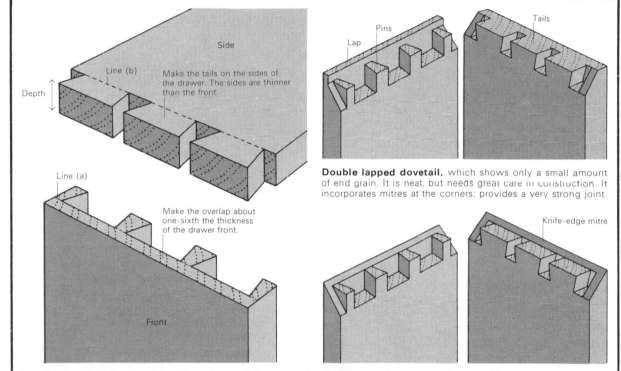

Make the tails on the sides of the drawer. The sides are thinner than the front.

Make the overlap about one-sixth the thickness of the drawer front.

Lapped dovetail, the ideal joint for the fronts of drawers and the corners of bookcases and sideboard carcases. Cut the tails in the sides and the pins in the overlapping pieces.

Double lapped dovetail, which shows only a small amount of end grain. It is neat, but needs great care in construction. It incorporates mitres at the corners; provides a very strong joint.

Secret, or mitre, dovetail, an uncommon joint used only in the highest-quality work. It takes a lot of practice to achieve an undamaged knife edge which will give the mitre a perfect fit.

Cutting the lap on a lapped dovetail joint. Mark the pins by placing the dovetailed side piece on top of the front piece and marking down the saw-cuts.

Hold the front piece upright in the vice and saw down the pins at 45° as far as possible. Be careful not to saw into the lap. Note that the waste is clearly marked.

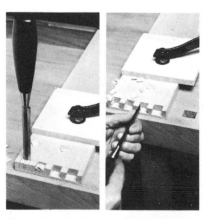

Chop out the waste, using a very small chisel to trim the corners covered by the overhang of the pins. Secure the wood firmly, preferably with a holdfast.

Fixing/1

Choosing the right hammer

Woodwork hammers are of two basic types, the claw and the cross-pein. A 450–570 gm. (16–20 oz.) claw hammer is a necessity as it drives and pulls out most nails. A cross-pein hammer is a useful addition for small pins and tacks.

Choose a hammer with a forged steel head as cheap cast ones tend to shatter.

Claw hammers have steel or wooden shafts, the best wooden ones being hickory. Steel shafts are stronger, but they have the slight disadvantage that the rubber or plastic grip becomes slippery in hot weather—wash the grip in cold water if this happens.

The cutaway section of the claw should taper to a fine V capable of pulling out fine pins.

The cross-pein hammer has a tapered end—the pein—on the head, for starting pins and tacks held between the fingers.

The pin hammer is the lightest version of the cross-pein hammer, and is used on pins which a heavier hammer would bend.

The pin push is a time saver for fixing hardboard or thin ply to framing. A panel pin fits into the end tube, which is held against the hardboard or ply and driven in by a push on the spring-loaded handle.

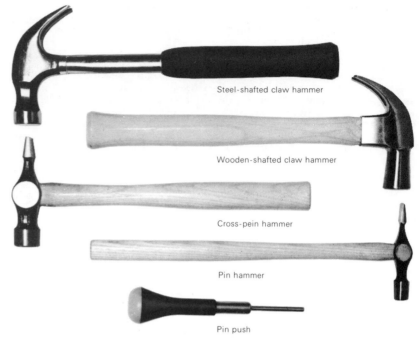

Steel-shafted claw hammer

Wooden-shafted claw hammer

Cross-pein hammer

Pin hammer

Pin push

Using hammers

Hitting a nail cleanly needs a firm stroke, pivoting from the elbow with no wrist movement. Grip the hammer handle near the end, not in the middle, and keep your eye on the nail. Start the nail by tapping, then swing from the elbow. Hit the nail with the handle at right angles to the nail at the moment of impact.

Good balance is essential in a hammer to obtain good results—the best test of a well-balanced claw hammer is if it comes to rest when stood on the claw.

A well-balanced claw hammer

The shape of the face—the striking part of the head—is important, too. It should be slightly domed so that if you hit a nail at an angle, the nail will still go in straight. The edge of the face should be very slightly chamfered.

Keep hammer faces clean and free from grease by occasionally rubbing them lightly on a flat sheet of sandpaper—a slipping hammer face causes nails to bend.

Preserve wooden handles by rubbing them at least once a year with raw linseed oil. Rub the oil in liberally with a rag for several minutes, then wipe the handle dry.

Take care not to touch finished surfaces with the plastic or rubber grip of a steel-shafted hammer, as it leaves black marks.

For various types of nails and their uses, see p. 48.

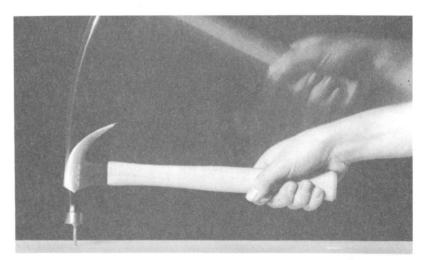

Keep the wrist straight as you strike; this will produce a clean hammer stroke.

Using the cross-pein. To start off short nails, tap them gently while held between the fingers until they stand on their own, then drive home with the hammer face.

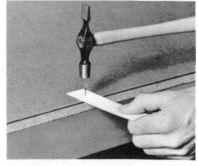

Tacking tip. Push very small pins through a piece of polythene and use it to hold them in position until started. When the pin is nearly home, tear the polythene away.

Punches

Use pin punches (they are sometimes known as nail sets) for driving headless nails or panel pins below the surface of timber, leaving a hole which is then filled and painted over so that no fixing is visible. Use them also to finish driving in nails where you do not want to mark the surface with the hammer head. Punches are usually 100 mm. (4 in.) long and point sizes vary in diameter from 1·5 to 4·5 mm. ($\frac{1}{16}$ to $\frac{3}{16}$ in.)—use a size slightly smaller than the diameter of the nail head.

Buy the square-headed rather than the round-headed type, which can roll away when put down on the workbench.

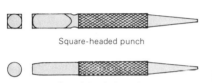

Square-headed punch

Round-headed punch

Punches are hollow ground at the tip so that they locate centrally on the nail head and stay there while you drive the nail home by tapping the punch with a hammer.

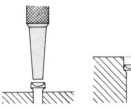

Use correct size punch   Drive nails in this far

Punch nail heads just below the surface —to roughly the same depth as the diameter of the nail head.

If you chip the end off a punch point, grind it back to above the chip line. This leaves the punch with a larger point than before, but it is still usable. You can restore the point to its original size by grinding down the tapered end along its length.

Removing nails

Partially driven nails are levered out with the claw of a claw hammer—hook the nail head in the V of the claw and remove the nail with a series of pulls. To pull out a long nail, slip a block of wood under the hammer head when the nail is half out and continue levering on that.

Use wood 'softening'—a scrap piece of wood—also to protect the surface you are levering on.

Pincers pull out nails that a claw hammer cannot—for example, a wire nail with the head off. A pair of 150 mm. (6 in.) pincers is the best all-round size.

For a lot of rough nail pulling, a nail puller—also known, significantly, as a wrecking bar—is useful. This is cleft at one end, for pulling nails, and has a chisel-type blade at the other, which is useful for raising floorboards.

If a nail defies all efforts to remove it, punch it in and fill the hole over it, or chisel away the wood round it until you can apply the pincers' jaws.

For maximum leverage, keep the handle working almost upright as you pull out the nails with the claw hammer.

To prevent damage to surfaces, place a piece of 'softening'—scrap wood—under the hammer head and lever on that.

Use pincers in a series of short, sharp pulls. If you remove the nail in one pull you leave a large, mis-shapen hole.

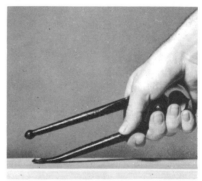

The fine claw on the end of a pincer handle slips under well-driven nails and pulls them up enough to let the jaws grip.

Replacing a hammer handle

Saw off and push out the old handle, file the top of the new one to fit into the hammer head, then cut two slots down from the top of the new handle, making them two-thirds of the head's depth.

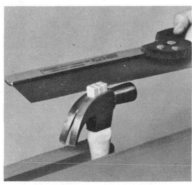

Drive the handle into the head and saw off the surplus wood. The handle must be dry and well-seasoned to stay tight—to ensure that it is, leave it in a barely warm oven for an hour before fitting.

Drive wedges—either hardwood home-made ones or metal bought ones—into the slots. When the handle is absolutely tight, file the top and the wedges flush with the head. Rub the handle with linseed oil.

Fixing/3

Types of nails

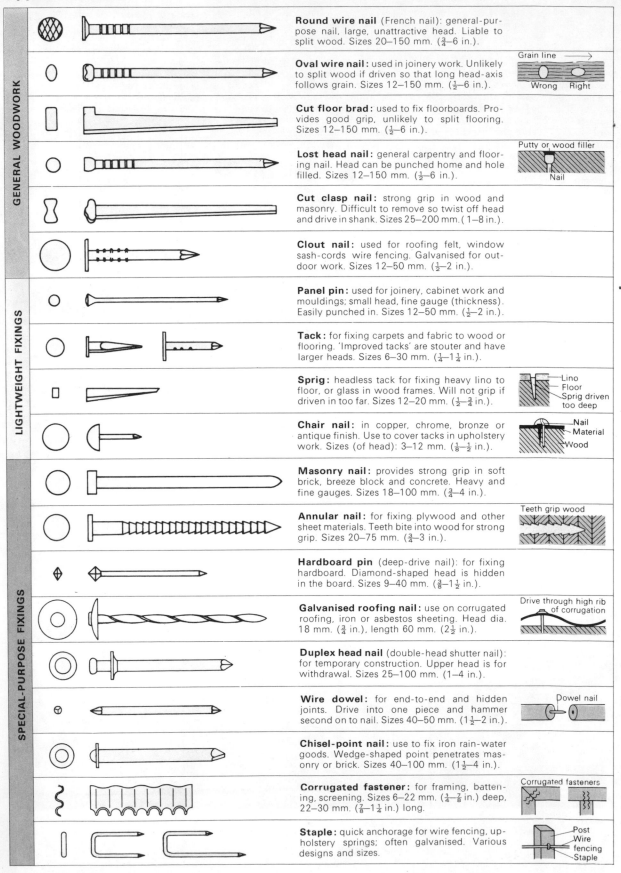

GENERAL WOODWORK

Round wire nail (French nail): general-purpose nail, large, unattractive head. Liable to split wood. Sizes 20–150 mm. ($\frac{3}{4}$–6 in.).

Oval wire nail: used in joinery work. Unlikely to split wood if driven so that long head-axis follows grain. Sizes 12–150 mm. ($\frac{1}{2}$–6 in.).

Grain line →
Wrong   Right

Cut floor brad: used to fix floorboards. Provides good grip, unlikely to split flooring. Sizes 12–150 mm. ($\frac{1}{2}$–6 in.).

Lost head nail: general carpentry and flooring nail. Head can be punched home and hole filled. Sizes 12–150 mm. ($\frac{1}{2}$–6 in.).

Putty or wood filler
Nail

Cut clasp nail: strong grip in wood and masonry. Difficult to remove so twist off head and drive in shank. Sizes 25–200 mm.(1–8 in.).

Clout nail: used for roofing felt, window sash-cords wire fencing. Galvanised for outdoor work. Sizes 12–50 mm. ($\frac{1}{2}$–2 in.).

LIGHTWEIGHT FIXINGS

Panel pin: used for joinery, cabinet work and mouldings; small head, fine gauge (thickness). Easily punched in. Sizes 12–50 mm. ($\frac{1}{2}$–2 in.).

Tack: for fixing carpets and fabric to wood or flooring. 'Improved tacks' are stouter and have larger heads. Sizes 6–30 mm. ($\frac{1}{4}$–1$\frac{1}{4}$ in.).

Sprig: headless tack for fixing heavy lino to floor, or glass in wood frames. Will not grip if driven in too far. Sizes 12–20 mm. ($\frac{1}{2}$–$\frac{3}{4}$ in.).

Lino
Floor
Sprig driven too deep

Chair nail: in copper, chrome, bronze or antique finish. Use to cover tacks in upholstery work. Sizes (of head): 3–12 mm. ($\frac{1}{8}$–$\frac{1}{2}$ in.).

Nail
Material
Wood

SPECIAL-PURPOSE FIXINGS

Masonry nail: provides strong grip in soft brick, breeze block and concrete. Heavy and fine gauges. Sizes 18–100 mm. ($\frac{3}{4}$–4 in.).

Annular nail: for fixing plywood and other sheet materials. Teeth bite into wood for strong grip. Sizes 20–75 mm. ($\frac{3}{4}$–3 in.).

Teeth grip wood

Hardboard pin (deep-drive nail): for fixing hardboard. Diamond-shaped head is hidden in the board. Sizes 9–40 mm. ($\frac{3}{8}$–1$\frac{1}{2}$ in.).

Galvanised roofing nail: use on corrugated roofing, iron or asbestos sheeting. Head dia. 18 mm. ($\frac{3}{4}$ in.), length 60 mm. (2$\frac{1}{2}$ in.).

Drive through high rib of corrugation

Duplex head nail (double-head shutter nail): for temporary construction. Upper head is for withdrawal. Sizes 25–100 mm. (1–4 in.).

Wire dowel: for end-to-end and hidden joints. Drive into one piece and hammer second on to nail. Sizes 40–50 mm. (1$\frac{1}{2}$–2 in.).

Dowel nail

Chisel-point nail: use to fix iron rain-water goods. Wedge-shaped point penetrates masonry or brick. Sizes 40–100 mm. (1$\frac{1}{2}$–4 in.).

Corrugated fastener: for framing, battening, screening. Sizes 6–22 mm. ($\frac{1}{4}$–$\frac{7}{8}$ in.) deep, 22–30 mm. ($\frac{7}{8}$–1$\frac{1}{4}$ in.) long.

Corrugated fasteners

Staple: quick anchorage for wire fencing, upholstery springs; often galvanised. Various designs and sizes.

Post
Wire fencing
Staple

How many nails?

Nails are sold by weight, and the number in a given weight is dependent upon their length. Finishes are generally bright mild steel, blued or black iron, or galvanised for outdoor jobs. Popular sizes of special-purpose nails and tacks are available in packages when only a small number is needed; larger nails, used in woodwork, are less expensive purchased by weight.

Approximate number of metric nails in a half kilo (imperial size nails per pound in brackets)

Length of nails	mm. in.	12 (½)	20 (¾)	25 (1)	30 (1¼)	40 (1½)	45 (1¾)	50 (2)	60 (2¼)	65 (2½)	75 (3)	90 (3½)	100 (4)	125 (5)	150 (6)
Round wire nail		—	1950 (1765)	890 (800)	585 (460)	375 (350)	300 (275)	180 (165)	140 (135)	135 (125)	77 (70)	50 (45)	40 (35)	27 (25)	16 (15)
Oval wire nail		3750 (3360)	2200 (2040)	1275 (1150)	760 (670)	460 (425)	325 (300)	230 (210)	160 (150)	110 (100)	60 (55)	44 (40)	33 (30)	22 (20)	16 (15)
Cut clasp nail		—	—	680 (620)	440 (390)	300 (280)	210 (200)	165 (150)	120 (110)	100 (90)	60 (55)	38 (35)	27 (25)	16 (15)	11 (10)
Lost head nail		4160 (3740)	2300 (2070)	1300 (1180)	760 (680)	500 (465)	315 (295)	235 (215)	160 (150)	110 (100)	66 (60)	50 (45)	38 (35)	22 (20)	16 (15)
Clout nail		1250 (1080)	540 (500)	375 (340)	360 (320)	270 (250)	160 (150)	130 (120)	—	—	—	—	—	—	—
Panel pin		4700 (4200)	2250 (2100)	1430 (1290)	1100 (985)	735 (670)	—	385 (350)	—	—	—	—	—	—	—

Nailing wood to wood

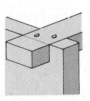

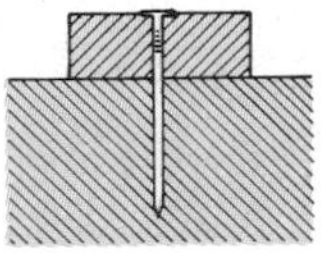

Use nails 2½ to 3 times longer than the thickness of the timber they must hold. Always nail light work to heavy.

Clench-nail for strong joints. Drive nails from opposite directions and bend the points into the wood.

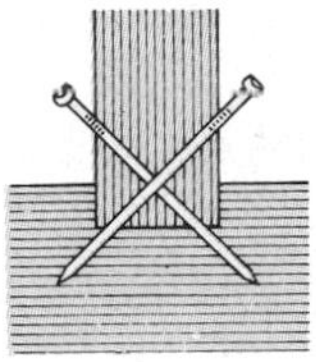

Skew-nail joints meeting at right angles. A housing joint is strongest and keeps the parts steady.

Use a cramp to steady a frame when skew-nailing flat joints. The first nail will hold while the second is driven.

Dovetail nailing grips better when driving into end grain. Drive staggered nails at opposing angles.

Avoid nailing into the same grain-line or the wood will split. Use square-shank nails to prevent splitting.

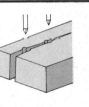

Avoid splitting end fixings by cutting wood overlength. Nail it in place before sawing off the excess.

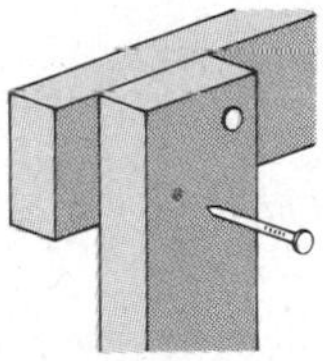

Avoid nailing into hardwood. If nails *must* be used, bore guide holes slightly smaller than the nail shank.

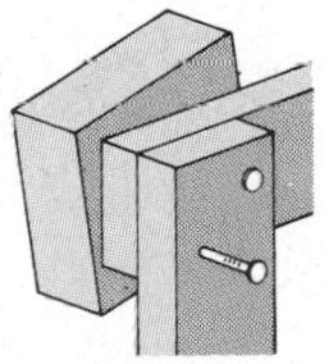

Prevent bouncing when nailing unsupported wood by holding a heavy block against the free side of the work.

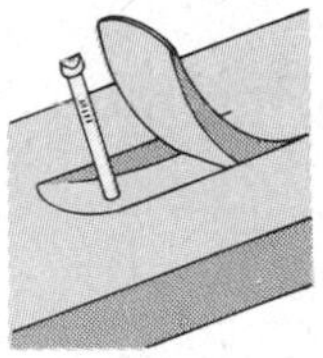

Secret nailing: chisel up a wood sliver and drive a nail into the recess. Glue the sliver back in position.

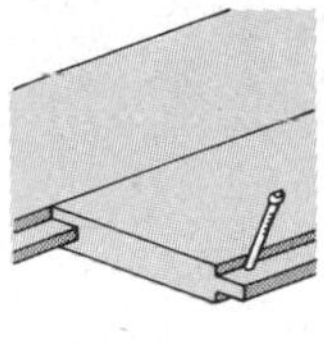

Secret-nail into floorboards by driving through tongue and shoulder. Angle nails to keep boards tight.

Push small nails and tacks through a thin cardboard holder so that fingers can be kept clear of the hammer.

Nailing wood to masonry

Use the correct length of masonry nail when fixing to brick, concrete or breeze block. If a nail penetrates more than 15–20 mm. (⅝–¾ in.) into the brickwork, its grip is weakened. Drive nails into the workpiece before applying it to the wall. When fixing to plastered brick, add the thickness of plaster to the workpiece width when deciding nail length.

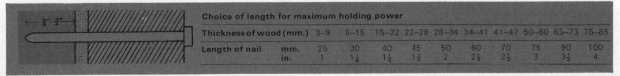

	Choice of length for maximum holding power									
Thickness of wood (mm.)	3–9	9–15	15–22	22–28	28–34	34–41	41–47	50–60	63–73	75–85
Length of nail mm. / in.	25 / 1	30 / 1¼	40 / 1½	45 / 1¾	50 / 2	60 / 2¼	70 / 2½	75 / 3	90 / 3½	100 / 4

Fixing/5

Using screwdrivers

Screwdrivers are among the commonest tools—and among the most commonly abused.

Always take care to use a screwdriver whose tip fits exactly into the slot in the screw head. Too wide a blade damages the wood as you screw in; too narrow a blade, or one which is rounded at the end, chews up the slot. Even if you manage to get the screw in with an undersized blade, it will look unsightly and be difficult to get out.

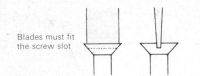

Blades must fit the screw slot

When using a screwdriver always keep the blade square in the slot—think of the screw as part of the screwdriver blade until it is driven home.

Always keep the tips of screwdrivers ground square and tapering evenly to the edge. To prevent marking wood when driving in countersunk screws, file off the corners of the blade.

If you are faced with extracting a screw with a damaged slot, try to move it with the longest screwdriver you have—the longer the screwdriver the more force it exerts. You may shift the screw by heating it with a soldering iron, allowing it to expand, then contract. If all else fails, drill the screw out down the centre and fill the hole.

Pozidriv screws, which have cross-shaped slots in the head, must be fixed with special screwdrivers whose blades match the slot—ordinary screwdrivers will not drive them home properly.

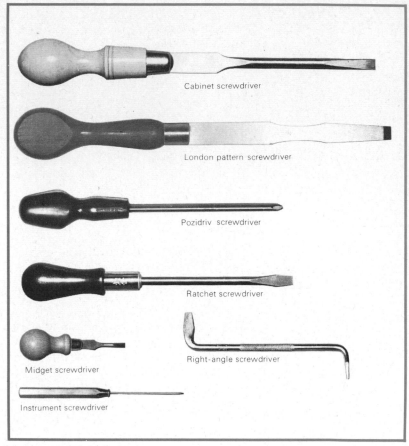

Cabinet screwdriver

London pattern screwdriver

Pozidriv screwdriver

Ratchet screwdriver

Right-angle screwdriver

Midget screwdriver

Instrument screwdriver

Screwdriver types. The cabinet pattern is a general bench tool; the London pattern is similar, but has an oval grip. Ratchet drivers cut out the need to change grip continually as you work. The midget and right-angle types get into awkward corners. Instrument screwdrivers are for fine screws. For Pozidriv screws use Pozidriv drivers only.

Pump-action screwdrivers

These fix screws fast by converting a downward push into a rotary action which drives in or withdraws a screw according to the ratchet setting.

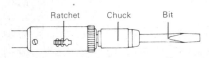

Ratchet   Chuck   Bit

If a pump driver is fitted with a lock, store it locked in the closed position

They can be used with a variety of interchangeable blades of different sizes and patterns, as well as reamers for starting screw holes in soft wood.

Their disadvantage is that they can do a lot of damage to the surrounding surface if they slip off the screw while you are pushing. Also, you cannot exert the force on a screw with them that you can with an orthodox screwdriver. In view of this, use a pump driver only on work where scarring does not matter, or can be patched.

Pump drivers are sold by a measurement which indicates the total extended length, the largest being 710 mm. (28 in.).

The pump action. Use two hands on the driver, make sure that the blade is squarely on the screw and lining up with it before pumping. A pump driver needs a lot of space in which to be worked.

Starting screws

Make a starting hole for any screw before using the screwdriver. A bradawl or gimlet does the job for screws up to No. 6 gauge. Larger ones need drilled holes (see table, p. 52, for details).

Bradawls have either square or tapered points; twist the blade into the wood by hand—if you hammer one it will be hard to get out.

Gimlets leave a protruding rim of wood round the hole they make, which should be smoothed off.

A screw always follows the hole made by a gimlet or bradawl—so make sure that it is straight.

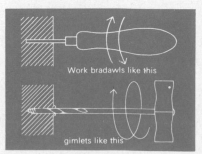

Work bradawls like this

gimlets like this

Types of screws

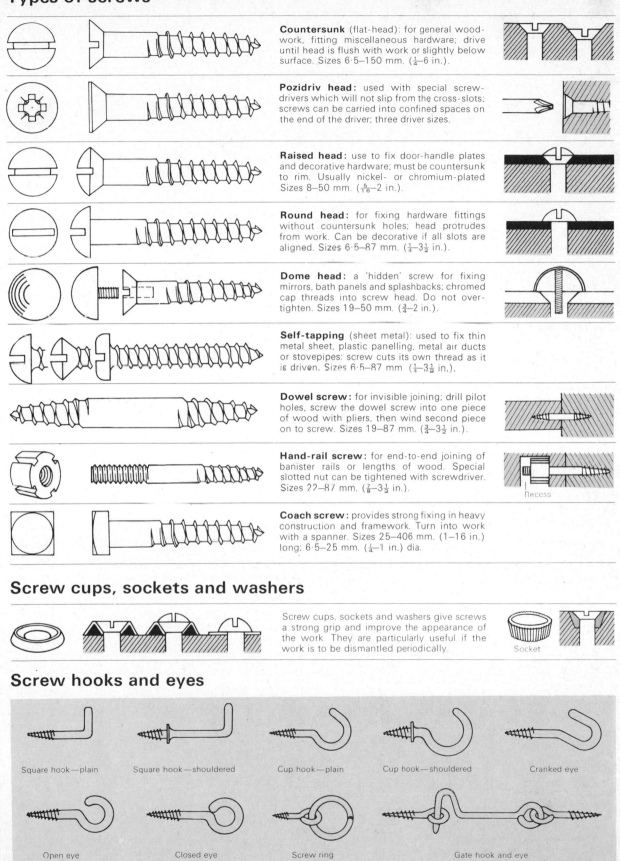

Countersunk (flat-head): for general wood-work, fitting miscellaneous hardware; drive until head is flush with work or slightly below surface. Sizes 6·5–150 mm. ($\frac{1}{4}$–6 in.).

Pozidriv head: used with special screw-drivers which will not slip from the cross-slots; screws can be carried into confined spaces on the end of the driver; three driver sizes.

Raised head: use to fix door-handle plates and decorative hardware; must be countersunk to rim. Usually nickel- or chromium-plated Sizes 8–50 mm. ($\frac{5}{16}$–2 in.).

Round head: for fixing hardware fittings without countersunk holes; head protrudes from work. Can be decorative if all slots are aligned. Sizes 6·5–87 mm. ($\frac{1}{4}$–3$\frac{1}{2}$ in.).

Dome head: a 'hidden' screw for fixing mirrors, bath panels and splashbacks; chromed cap threads into screw head. Do not over-tighten. Sizes 19–50 mm. ($\frac{3}{4}$–2 in.).

Self-tapping (sheet metal): used to fix thin metal sheet, plastic panelling, metal air ducts or stovepipes: screw cuts its own thread as it is driven. Sizes 6·5–87 mm ($\frac{1}{4}$–3$\frac{1}{2}$ in.).

Dowel screw: for invisible joining; drill pilot holes, screw the dowel screw into one piece of wood with pliers, then wind second piece on to screw. Sizes 19–87 mm. ($\frac{3}{4}$–3$\frac{1}{2}$ in.).

Hand-rail screw: for end-to-end joining of banister rails or lengths of wood. Special slotted nut can be tightened with screwdriver. Sizes 22–87 mm. ($\frac{7}{8}$–3$\frac{1}{2}$ in.).

Recess

Coach screw: provides strong fixing in heavy construction and framework. Turn into work with a spanner. Sizes 25–406 mm. (1–16 in.) long; 6·5–25 mm. ($\frac{1}{4}$–1 in.) dia.

Screw cups, sockets and washers

Screw cups, sockets and washers give screws a strong grip and improve the appearance of the work. They are particularly useful if the work is to be dismantled periodically.

Socket

Screw hooks and eyes

Square hook—plain

Square hook—shouldered

Cup hook—plain

Cup hook—shouldered

Cranked eye

Open eye

Closed eye

Screw ring

Gate hook and eye

Buying and using screws

Screws are made of mild steel, brass, copper, gun-metal or aluminium. Finishes can be black japanned, galvanised or plated with nickel, tin, zinc or chromium.

Length — Shank

The size of a screw is determined by the diameter of its shank (gauge), and the length from the rim of the head to the thread tip. Gauge numbers do not vary with screw length: a 25 mm. (1 in.) 8 gauge screw has the same size head and shank as a 76 mm. (3 in.) 8 gauge screw.

The most economic way to buy screws is by the box of 100, 200 or 500.

Two holes for thread and shank clearance are needed before screws are driven in, and for this purpose it is useful to have a screw gauge available.

Make the pilot hole slightly smaller than the screw gauge so that the threads of the screw will bite into the wood; and make the clearance hole slightly larger than the gauge to allow room for the shank. If you are making a number of holes for the same size screw, it is advisable to mark the depth required, especially for the shank, with a piece of white adhesive tape stuck round the drill.

Use a countersink bit to shape the tops of clearance holes when they are to receive countersunk screws.

Softwoods require smaller pilot holes than hardwoods, and clearance holes are not needed when screws smaller than number 7 gauge are used.(see table).

Lubricate screws with wax or candle-grease before driving. When using brass screws in hardwood, lower resistance by first driving a steel screw of the same size as the brass screw.

What gauge—what length?

The table shows the length of screws available in each gauge group and, at the bottom of each gauge number column, what size drill is needed to make clearance and thread holes. Hole diameters are larger for hardwoods than softwoods.

Using a brace and bit

A swing brace bores holes fast and accurately, and can be used with bits which drill bigger holes than you can get with a power drill.

The vital measurement on a brace is its 'sweep'—the radius of the circle described by the grip. A wide sweep gives more power, but makes the brace harder to handle in confined places. A 250 mm. (10 in.) sweep is the best compromise.

A ratchet brace is better than a fixed one, as it allows drilling in confined places by working the grip to and fro through an arc instead of through a full circle.

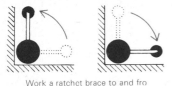

Work a ratchet brace to and fro in confined spaces

When drilling, avoid splitting the wood as you near the end of the hole in this way: drill until the point of the bit just breaks through on the other side, turn the wood round and resume drilling with the point in the hole it made from the other side.

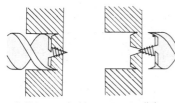

Drill from each side to prevent splitting

If you cannot drill from both sides, take the last few turns gently to minimise splitting, or place a block behind the hole and drill through into it.

Fit the bit with a depth-stop if you are drilling to a fixed depth. A depth-stop can be bought or made from a piece of drilled-out scrap wood or rubber tubing which fits over the bit and stops it from going deeper than you want. Insulating tape stuck round the bit also provides a guide.

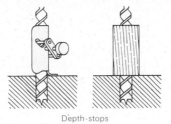

Depth-stops

Bits

Only square-ended bits can be used with a brace. They are fitted by inserting them into the jaws of the chuck, which is held in one hand while the brace is turned clockwise to tighten the jaws.

If jaws start failing to grip after long use,

Drilling accurately. Sight the bit against a try-square—or better still, get someone else to do it—to ensure straight drilling. For horizontal drilling, hold the mushroom handle against the body.

you can buy a replaceable set: fit them by unscrewing the chuck to its fullest extent, easing out the old ones and putting the new set in with the open (wider apart) end facing out of the chuck.

Bits suitable for brace use include:

Jennings pattern—the commonest type, whose spiral keeps the hole straight during deep drilling.

Solid centre pattern—fast but slightly less accurate.

Expansive bit—has adjustable cutter for holes of different sizes. May wander on deep holes: unsuitable for material less than 9 mm. ($\frac{3}{8}$ in.) thick, and hardwood.

Forstner bit—extremely accurate but requires a lot of pressure to keep going; drills flat-bottomed holes.

Centre bit—first class for cutting plywood; wanders on long holes.

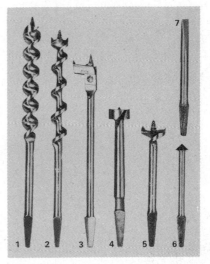

Bit types: 1. Jennings pattern. **2.** Solid centre. **3.** Expansive bit. **4.** Forstner bit. **5.** Centre bit. **6.** Countersink. **7.** Screwdriver. The centre bit pattern is the most common.

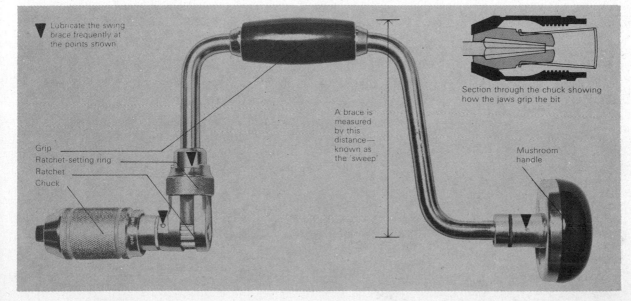

Lubricate the swing brace frequently at the points shown

Section through the chuck showing how the jaws grip the bit

Grip
Ratchet-setting ring
Ratchet
Chuck

A brace is measured by this distance—known as the 'sweep'

Mushroom handle

Fixing/9

Sharpening bits

Using a 100 mm. (4 in.) needle file with a medium cut, you can sharpen Jennings pattern, expansive and centre bits yourself. The procedure is to restore the cutting angle, filing off as little metal as possible.

Send Forstner bits back to the tool shop or manufacturer for resharpening. Masonry bits need special resharpening equipment and it is easiest to replace them,

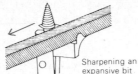

Sharpening an expansive bit

though some manufacturers provide a sharpening service. Screwdriver bits can be reground. Countersink bits must be replaced when worn.

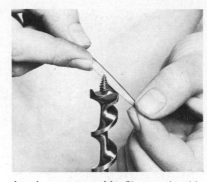

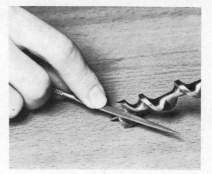

Jennings pattern bit. Sharpen the side (wing) cutters from the inside only, filing with the slight curve of the cutting edge. Take care not to file down one side cutter so that it is lower than the other. Sharpen the horizontal cutters on the top only, following the original angle. Only file the underneath very lightly—just enough to remove any burr. Centre bits, which usually have only one side cutter and one horizontal cutter, are sharpened similarly.

Wheelbrace

The wheelbrace, used with twist drills, is for cutting holes up to 8 mm. ($\frac{5}{16}$ in.) dia. in wood, metal and plastic. It is obviously much slower than the electric drill, but it is more easily controlled and can get into places where an electric drill cannot.

It is usually sold with an additional, removable side handle, which is used only when more pressure and control are needed.

In such situations, press the main handle into the stomach, to give pressure, and use the side handle to prevent the brace from twisting as you use the turning handle.

If drilling upright, grip the main handle in the fist and press down on that with the chest to get more pressure.

drive-wheel need cleaning, remove the screw holding the turning handle, lift the handle from the centre shaft, and take the wheel off.

When reversing the procedure to refit the wheel, you must ensure that the pinions mesh with it before you finally fit the handle.

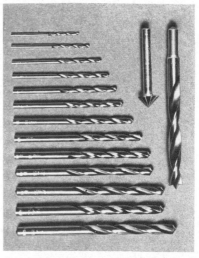

Any twist drill or countersink with a shank size up to 6·5 mm. ($\frac{1}{4}$ in.) can be used with a wheelbrace. The usual range is 0·5–6·5 mm. ($\frac{1}{32}$–$\frac{1}{4}$ in.). Dowel bits (on right) can also be used.

Back cap   Chuck body   Jaws

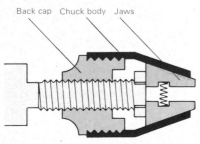

Chucks fitted to wheelbraces contain three self-centring jaws to take round-shanked bits or countersinks.

After a great deal of use, the jaws may become worn and fail to grip, but replacements can be bought and are easily fitted in a few minutes: remove the chuck from the brace by unscrewing as if opening the chuck jaws, hold the knurled body of the chuck in a vice and unscrew the back cap; remove the chuck body from the vice and tap it so that the old jaws fall out.

Drop in the new set with the points first and squeezed together. Push them home; refit the back cap to the chuck body and screw it back on to the brace.

Wheelbraces need little maintenance. Apply a little oil occasionally to the gears, the chuck and the oil hole in the casting just above the chuck. Should the main

Main handle

Turning handle

Side handle

Main drive-wheel

Pinion

Chuck

Grip the main handle on the wheelbrace in the fist—thumb towards the wheel for horizontal drilling, thumb on top for vertical drilling. Body pressure is usually only necessary when drilling metal.

How an electric drill works

Electrically powered tools suitable for home repairs and improvements range from the basic electric drill to more specialist and costly items such as radial arm saws and mechanical routers.

From the average householder's point of view, the most satisfactory investment for general work and repairs is an electric drill power unit which can be used to drive a range of attachments. These can be bought as and when the need arises.

Drills are usually graded by their chuck capacity or, in other words, the maximum diameter of twist bit shank which can be secured in the chuck. This is usually 6·5 or 8 mm. ($\frac{1}{4}$ or $\frac{5}{16}$ in.) but can be greater on heavy-duty professional models.

The table below, which gives suitable drill speeds for various jobs, shows that two-speed or variable-speed power units

are more flexible than the less expensive single-speed units and are thus a wiser investment.

The cost of a single-speed unit together with a speed-reducing device is usually higher than for a variable-speed drill. Reducers for single-speed drills can be either electronic or mechanical.

Electronic reducers are fitted to the supply cable and allow the required speed to be selected by knob or dial control.

Mechanical reducers are fitted to the tools themselves, either instead of or into the chuck. Neither is as convenient to use as a variable-speed drill.

Most power tools are now fitted with double-pole switches which cut off both live and negative cores in the supply cable, thus completely isolating the motor electrically. When the switch is pressed to the

'on' position, current passes to one of the field coils and from there to the armature via the carbon brushes and commutator.

The armature main shaft speed of 20,000 revolutions per minute is geared down to approximately 3000 rpm. This reduction of speed increases the 'torque', or driving force. A fan is fitted internally to lower working temperatures.

Light-duty sleeve bearings are fitted to some power tools but better-quality models have needle or ball bearings, which are more suitable for continuous use.

Electrical connections in the motor are usually welded. The soldered connections on some models may fail if excessive heat or sparking occurs, for instance as a result of overloading or worn or clogged carbon brushes.

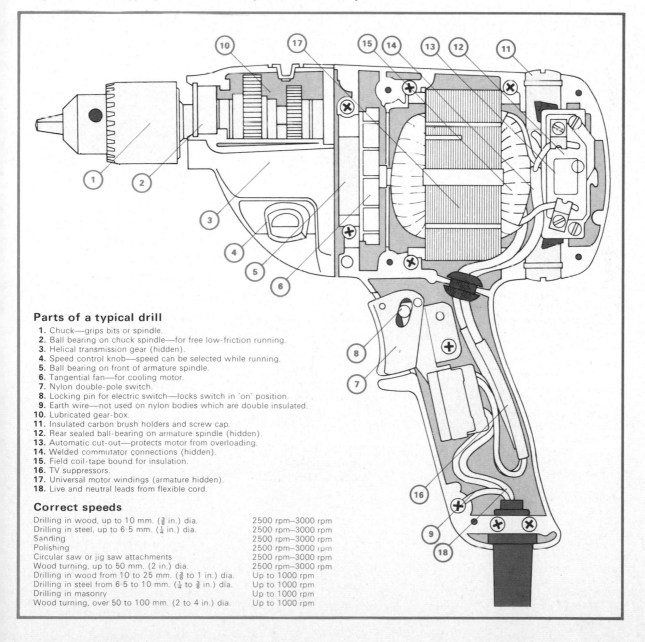

Parts of a typical drill

1. Chuck—grips bits or spindle.
2. Ball bearing on chuck spindle—for free low-friction running.
3. Helical transmission gear (hidden).
4. Speed control knob—speed can be selected while running.
5. Ball bearing on front of armature spindle.
6. Tangential fan—for cooling motor.
7. Nylon double-pole switch.
8. Locking pin for electric switch—locks switch in 'on' position.
9. Earth wire—not used on nylon bodies which are double insulated.
10. Lubricated gear-box.
11. Insulated carbon brush holders and screw cap.
12. Rear sealed ball-bearing on armature spindle (hidden).
13. Automatic cut-out—protects motor from overloading.
14. Welded commutator connections (hidden).
15. Field coil-tape bound for insulation.
16. TV suppressors.
17. Universal motor windings (armature hidden).
18. Live and neutral leads from flexible cord.

Correct speeds

Drilling in wood, up to 10 mm. ($\frac{3}{8}$ in.) dia.	2500 rpm–3000 rpm
Drilling in steel, up to 6·5 mm. ($\frac{1}{4}$ in.) dia.	2500 rpm–3000 rpm
Sanding	2500 rpm–3000 rpm
Polishing	2500 rpm–3000 rpm
Circular saw or jig saw attachments	2500 rpm–3000 rpm
Wood turning, up to 50 mm. (2 in.) dia.	2500 rpm–3000 rpm
Drilling in wood from 10 to 25 mm. ($\frac{3}{8}$ to 1 in.) dia.	Up to 1000 rpm
Drilling in steel from 6·5 to 10 mm. ($\frac{1}{4}$ to $\frac{3}{8}$ in.) dia.	Up to 1000 rpm
Drilling in masonry	Up to 1000 rpm
Wood turning, over 50 to 100 mm. (2 to 4 in.) dia.	Up to 1000 rpm

Fixing/11

Maintenance of drills

A drop in speed while a power tool is in use, usually accompanied by a lowering of motor pitch, is a sign of overloading. To avoid the damage which this can cause, remove the tool from the work and run it at full revs for a few seconds before using it again. This not only avoids abuse but also helps to reduce overheating.

Automatic cut-outs, which come into operation when overloading occurs, are fitted on some models. After a stoppage, these should be reset to 'on' only after removing the tool from the work.

Examine the carbon brushes periodically. These can be cleaned with turps substitute and, if necessary, with a very fine '0000' abrasive paper. To ensure correct replacement, note the position of the brushes before removing them. Replace badly or unevenly worn brushes and have the entire tool overhauled by the manufacturer or his agent.

Undue commutator sparking indicates an electrical fault—leave this repair to a qualified expert.

Occasionally open up the gearbox, clean out the old grease and repack with the lubricant recommended by the maker.

Double-insulated tools are quite safe to use with the two-core cables provided, but tools with three-core cables must always be connected to a three-pin plug and socket.

Always use a drill with the cable hitched over your shoulder, out of the way.

Unless chuck keys are kept in the holders provided or tied to the supply cable, they are easily mislaid. A spare key is an invaluable accessory.

Repacking the gearbox. The front of the drill is unscrewed to expose the gearbox. Wipe away all the old grease and repack with a high-flashpoint grease—manufacturers usually supply the correct grease for repacking. Change grease at least annually.

Types of bit

Twist bits: sold singly or in sets of graded sizes for general use with power tools. Although designed for metalwork, they are more often used for drilling timber. 'Green' softwoods tend to clog these drills—retract them frequently and clean out the waste compacted in the grooves with a nail or awl.

Auger bits: strictly woodworking tools. Centre spurs allow precise centring so that these bits will drill accurately in any grain direction.

Dowel bits: for flat-bottomed holes, using power tool at full speed. They are not as accurate as auger bits, especially when drilling into end grain.

Countersinking bits: for 'belling out' the mouths of already drilled screw holes, allowing countersunk screw heads to be sunk flush with or slightly below the timber surface. Various sizes available.

Drill-countersinkers: combination bits which first drill a screw hole to the depth and diameter required and then bell out the mouth for the screw head.

Power bore bits: specially made for drilling larger diameter holes in timber, using power tools at full speed. One of the most accurate drills available.

Shell and parrot-nosed augers: long bits for drilling holes in standard lamp poles etc. on a lathe. They can be used freehand if a pilot hole is drilled first. When doing this, never drill more than 50 mm. (2 in.) at a time without retracting the bit and cleaning out the waste.

Slotting and shaping bits: patent tools with rasp-type shanks, used for elongating or widening holes previously made with a normal bit.

Hole saws: combination of centre pilot bit and ring-shaped saw for cutting large diameter holes through timber, plywood and hardboard up to 6·5 mm. ($\frac{1}{4}$ in.) thick. Normally supplied with ring-saws of different diameters. Efficiency can be improved by filing down every other tooth.

Masonry bits: twist bits with special alloy tips for drilling through brick, concrete, tiles, etc.

Spear point bits: for drilling through glass and mirrors. Use at low speeds and keep the work lubricated with turps substitute; keep a pool of it in a putty ring around the hole.

Flat bits: for general-purpose, large-hole boring.

After use, rub down bits with steel wool and wipe with a thin oil. Waste wood compacted into the grooves will cause bits to clog, overheat, lose their temper and so become useless.

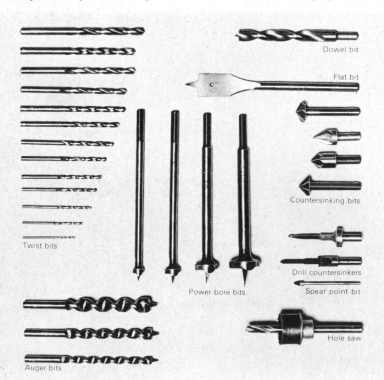

Twist bits

Power bore bits

Auger bits

Dowel bit

Flat bit

Countersinking bits

Drill countersinkers

Spear point bit

Hole saw

Drilling square

Always ensure that you are drilling at right angles to the work surface.

One way to do this is to line up your bit with an up-ended try-square and, if possible, enlist a helper to tell you when you are wandering off the vertical.

A surer alternative is to use one of the many types of jig now available.

Dowelling jigs, which give accurate siting and drilling of holes to take wooden dowels, range from the simple drilled metal block to more complicated (and accurate) calibrated types such as the Stanley Doweling Jig.

To position dowel holes when no jig is at hand, mark out their centres on one of the two members to be joined and drive pins into the marks. Nip the heads until only 5 mm. ($\frac{1}{4}$ in.) of shank is protruding, then position and press the other member down on to the first. Separate the members, remove the pins and then drill the dowel holes, using the pin marks as centres.

When using a power drill, make sure that the material to be drilled is firm and steady.

Large pieces usually present little difficulty and can be held firmly by hand, but always hold small pieces in a vice or cramp them to the drill table or bench This will overcome the tendency of the cutting drill to suddenly snatch at the piece and spin it round.

The way to ensure 100 per cent accuracy for any drilling job is to use a purpose-made horizontal drill stand.

Ensure that you buy one into which your drill fits—which usually means it must be the same make, though the Arcoy stand will accommodate most makes.

With a stand you can widen your scope considerably. Mortise cutting is easy: you mark out the mortise and drill out most of the waste to a finely controlled depth, finishing the slot off with a chisel. You can buy a mortising attachment which does the whole job.

Most drill stands are fitted with stops that can be adjusted for drilling to predetermined depths. Dowelling holes will also be true and square when done with a drill in a stand.

Plug-cutter attached to drill

A simple attachment for use with a drill stand is the Stanley plug-cutter, which allows you to conceal screw or other holes in finished surfaces: cut a plug from a matching piece of timber, drive the screw well below the surface and glue in the plug, sanding it flush.

Other useful drill attachments are the Black and Decker right-angle speed changer, which doubles or halves the speed of the drill as well as allowing you to work round corners; and the flexible drive attachment for getting at really awkward places.

Right-angle drive
replaces chuck

One word of warning about attachments: check that an attachment fits your drill before buying, as most makers' accessories fit only their make of drill.

Flexible drive

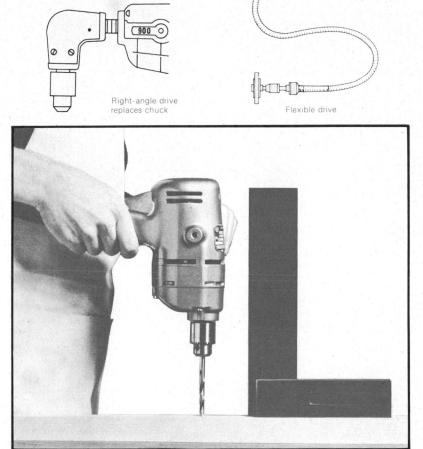

Drilling accurately. If you have no jig, you will need a helper to ensure that you are drilling at right angles to the surface by sighting the bit against a try-square.

Dowelling. True, matching holes, best drilled with a jig, are essential.

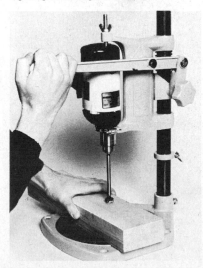

Drill stand. The bit is fed into the work accurately and evenly by lever-control.

Finishing/1

How to use abrasive papers

Abrasive papers are made with a variety of coatings, such as granules of glass, garnet, emery, silicone-carbide and flint.

'Sandpaper' as such does not exist, this being the misleading name given to glass-paper. Glass-paper and garnet-paper are used for smoothing bare wood to a fine finish. Garnet-paper lasts longer and gives a cleaner cut.

Silicone-carbide paper is better known as 'wet-or-dry', referring to the two ways in which it can be used. When dry it is used like garnet or glass-paper. When wet, it is for cleaning off and smoothing down paint. It will last a long time wet, and gives a very smooth finish, though it does leave a sludgy mess which has to be washed off. It is suitable for rubbing down paintwork on both metal (such as car bodies) and wood. The paper should only be kept damp—not running with water.

Emery-paper is for finishing metal only.

All these papers come in ranges varying from coarse to fine. With all of them, the procedure is to start with a coarse paper and work down through the finer grades until the required smoothness of finish is reached.

A fine finish can only be achieved with a fine paper—a coarse paper will not give a good finish, no matter how worn it is. On hardwood, use a cabinet scraper rather than abrasive paper—dust produced by sanding clogs the grain.

Always use abrasive paper with a cork sanding-block. These only cost a few pence each and are vital for an even finish, as they hold the whole of the paper flat against the surface at the same time. If you use the paper in the palm of your hand, it will only cut where the hand is pressing it against the wood.

If you have to smooth down a shaped edge or a moulding, it is worth cutting a matching-shaped block out of cork or wood, and using the paper wrapped around that. To get the block to match the moulding exactly, cut it roughly to shape then put a piece of abrasive paper on the moulding and rub the block to shape on it.

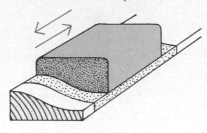

Shaping a block to a moulding

Sanding tips

Damp wood will not clean up to a good finish with any kind of abrasive paper.

Always store abrasive paper in a warm cupboard—damp paper is useless.

If paper becomes clogged during use, clear it by running the back of the sheet over the edge of the bench. This will also make the paper more flexible and therefore less liable to crack.

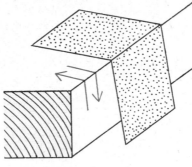

Cleaning clogged paper

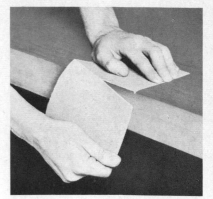

Tear paper against a sharp edge such as the edge of the bench. A sheet of abrasive paper divides into six equal parts, to fit around a standard cork sanding-block.

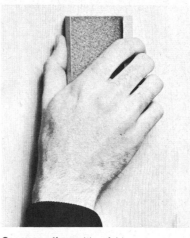

Start sanding with a fairly coarse paper, working down through the grades and finishing off with a fine paper. Always work with the grain.

Files

Have at least one file handy for odd smoothing jobs, such as rounding off corners, trimming laminate bonded to ply or blockboard, and flattening a combination of wood and metal. A 250 mm. (10 in.) long flat file, with a fine cut, is a good all-round pattern. Use it two-handed, at waist level. Cut on the forward stroke, taking care not to work with a rocking motion as this will give a curved surface.

Floor scrapers

For smoothing floors and other similar large areas, use scrapers with metal or wooden handles, such as the Skarsten scraper.

Floors can be smoothed more easily by doing the main area with a hired commercial sander, but a scraper is still needed for edges and corners where the sander cannot reach.

Scrapers with replaceable blades are available in smaller sizes for a variety of smoothing jobs, and they are easier to handle than cabinet scrapers over long periods.

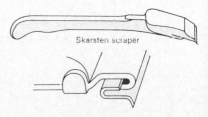

Skarsten scraper

Blade slots into lip

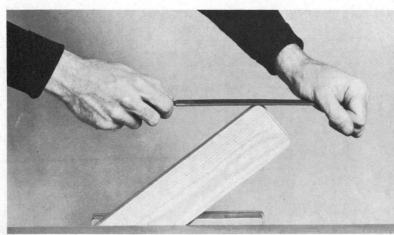

Preparation

Correct preparation is essential for any wood finish. Modern clear finishes in particular accentuate scratches and other imperfections, if not removed. Get as fine a finish as possible with the cutting tools to keep sanding to a minimum, especially on hardwood. After planing wood, or scraping a veneered surface with a cabinet scraper, sand carefully to remove any tool marks, torn grain or glue.

For sanding, wrap the paper around a flat cork block (see p. 58); an odd scrap of wood is not really suitable. Garnet or Lubrisil papers require less effort than glass-paper, but they cost more and are not always readily obtainable.

Sand with a firm, moderate pressure, and keep the block in a straight line with the direction of the grain.

Remember that you are trying to get the surface flat as well as smooth, so occasionally alternate the angle of the block to the work but continue to work it in the direction of the grain.

Sunlight darkens newly finished wood. On no account leave anything standing on a freshly sanded surface; it will cause a light patch which must be re-sanded.

Veneers are exceptionally thin, so take great care when scraping or sanding, particularly on the corners.

Work down through three grades of abrasive paper, starting with a reasonably coarse grade, following with a medium grade and finishing with a fine paper.

After sanding, use a fine brush to remove grit and dust from the surface of the work, brushing in the direction of the grain to ensure that crevices are clear.

Power orbital sanders are useful for finishing but require experience to use,

especially on veneers. Do not use sanding discs or portable belt sanders unless the work is to be painted.

Fill irremovable blemishes, such as panel pin holes, splits and small knots, with a stopping such as Brummer Yellow Label, which can be bought in a range of colours to match most timbers.

Press the stopping into the hole, taking care not to spread it into the grain beyond the immediate blemish. Let the stopping dry, then sand it flat.

If a small item is to be finished, protect the bench from becoming stained by covering it with hardboard; if the work is large,

raise it off the floor on blocks or place it on sawing stools.

Finishes cannot be applied successfully in all temperatures: 18–21°C (64–70°F) is ideal for most operations. Do not attempt finishing in cold or damp conditions.

Do not carry out staining and colouring in artificial light. Plenty of daylight is advisable, but not direct sunlight.

Before starting, sand off sweaty finger marks and have plenty of clean, non-fluffy cotton cloth available.

Cleanliness is essential, so remove all dust from the bench and floor before starting work.

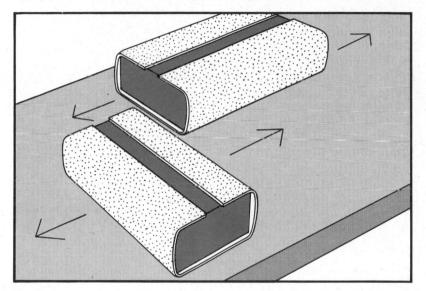

Sanding: always work with the grain— one scratch across the grain takes a long time to remove or, if left, shows up like a knife cut underneath polish

Staining

Before finishing timber, you may want to stain it. It is better not to stain new work; nearly all timbers are more attractive when left natural, and the process of staining is tricky unless you have had experience. But it may be necessary when repairing old furniture or when a new item has to be matched with existing furniture.

Stains are readily available, in a variety of shades, from ironmongers and do-it-yourself shops. If possible, select the type of stain recommended by the manufacturer of the finish you intend to use. With so many chemical finishes available, this eliminates the risk of a reaction setting in between the stain and the finish.

If in doubt, choose a water stain. This

will not cause a chemical reaction, but the wood will require sanding after application of the stain as water stains raise the grain.

Before staining, experiment on an odd piece of the same timber, carefully sanded, to make sure that you have the shade required. Allow the stain to dry, then apply a coat of finish; this will further darken and enrich the colour.

To achieve a particular shade, stains can be mixed, provided they are of the same type and from the same manufacturer. Mix enough at one time to complete the whole job, as it is difficult to mix two batches to exactly the same shade.

Application: working quickly with a soft,

dry, non-fluffy cloth or brush, apply a liberal, even coat over the whole surface, taking care to work in the direction of the grain.

Wipe off the excess with a clean, dry cloth, working evenly and with the grain, before the stain has dried. When working on a large area, take care that drying out does not occur before the whole surface has been covered with stain, otherwise the final colouring will be uneven.

When dry, wipe the surface again with another dry cloth before applying any finish.

Take care not to spill drops of stain on untreated surfaces as these will penetrate deeply and show as dark patches.

Grain filling

Grain fillers fill the pores of the timber and give the finish a flat, mirror-like surface, as in French polishing. Today the tendency is to leave timber looking as natural as possible so that the texture of the grain can be seen and felt. For this reason, fillers are often dispensed with.

Fillers should not be used for oil, wax

or limed finishes, but they are advisable before French polishing and for some open-grained timbers, such as oak or rosewood, when a heavily brushed or sprayed lacquer is to be applied.

Application: use the grain filler recommended by the manufacturer of the finish that you intend using. Read the maker's

instructions: some fillers require thinning.

Apply the shade required liberally by brush or rag, working it into the surface with a circular motion and finishing off across the grain; wipe off the surplus and allow to dry.

When thoroughly hard and dry, sand lightly with the grain.

Finishing/3

Rubber disc and drum sanders

Sanding, always a tedious task, can be speeded up by the intelligent use of power tools. The most common attachment is the flexible rubber backing disc to which discs of abrasive paper are screwed. Disc sanders are also available as integral tools and as attachments to turning lathes.

Ideally, timber should always be sanded along the grain direction, and disc sanders inevitably break this golden rule. For this reason a more satisfactory appliance is the belt sander. This is usually an integral tool which consists of a moving abrasive belt tensioned between two drive rollers. The nearest equivalent in power tool attachments is the drum sander, which also allows with-the-grain sanding.

Because of their rotary action, sanding discs must be used very carefully to avoid undue of circular marking of the surface. It is usually best to complete the coarse sanding with a disc, working from coarse to medium grade abrasive papers, and then to complete the fine sanding by hand.

Never attempt to use the whole surface of the disc, as this will inevitably leave deep and difficult-to-remove circular marks.

Tilt the disc at an angle of 30° so that only one-third of its area is in contact with the work. Too much downward pressure may cause overloading. Keep the sanding action light, always working with a sweeping movement of the tool.

Disc sanders will not remove paint because the heat generated causes it to melt, forcing it further into the timber and clogging the abrasive paper. Avoid sanding over sharp edges which will snag and tear the sanding discs.

The drum sander, consisting of a foam-rubber wheel with an abrasive 'tyre', can be used on convex, concave and flat surfaces. Its action in removing waste is not as effective as the disc sander's but it does have the important advantage of being able to work in the direction of the grain.

The abrasive belt or tyre is held to the foam-rubber wheel with spots of non-hardening adhesive applied to the non-abrasive side. The bond tends to fail after some time. When the abrasive belt starts to slip, more adhesive must be applied. As with the disc sander, light pressure gives the best results.

Abrasives for use with power sanders include ordinary glass- or sandpapers and the garnet-papers which have better durability and performance. Even better are the more expensive aluminium oxide papers.

The printed numbers on the back of abrasive papers denote the number of grit particles per square inch. Thus a coarse '40' grade paper will have 40 particles in 25 mm. square (square inch) and a fine '80' paper 80. When ordering abrasive discs or belts, always state the grade numbers required. Store abrasives in a dry place as damp, and even atmospheric humidity, can make them useless.

The drum sander, an abrasive 'tyre' stretched over a foam-rubber wheel, can be used for finishing off curved surfaces.

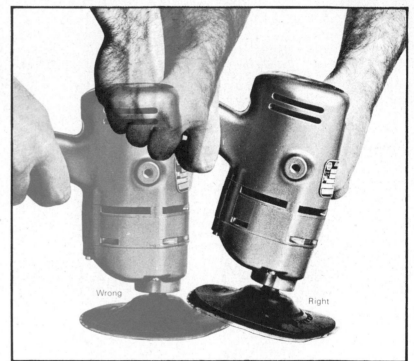

Wrong

Right

Do not use the full area of a sanding disc, as this will lead to deep circular marks which are difficult to remove. Instead, tilt the tool (as illustrated) using mainly the edge of the disc. Work over the surface with a sweeping action.

Orbital sanders

Orbital sanders are for fine finishing work only and should not be used for removing any appreciable quantity of material. The flat cushioned pad over which abrasive paper is stretched rotates in small circles of about 10 mm. ($\frac{3}{8}$ in.) dia. The tiny circular marks it leaves can only be detected under very close examination, but to this extent orbital sanders do not come up to careful hand sanding standards. They are, however, extremely useful for rubbing down and keying paintwork in preparation for extra coats.

Usually the weight of the tool on its own provides sufficient downward pressure, though it must be steadied by hand to prevent it skating about on the surface.

Abrasive paper is stretched over the pad by knurled rollers. These are turned with a screwdriver to admit and tension the paper.

Use the side handle on the drill when working with an orbital sander attachment. No downward pressure is needed.

Sanding discs

More accurate than the flexible rubber sanding disc is the rigid type, fitted to a power tool mounted on a bench stand accessory. Similar sanders are also available as attachments to universal woodworking machines. The main use of the rigid sanding disc is for producing smooth, perfectly level surfaces on woodwork.

To ease removal and replacement when worn, abrasive papers are stuck to the rigid backing disc with a non-hardening adhesive made for the purpose. This is spread on to the backing disc while it is rotating, and the abrasive disc is pressed on firmly when the tool is at rest. After peeling off a worn abrasive disc, skim off the remaining adhesive by holding a blunt strip of metal against the rotating disc.

Although a platform on which the work is rested is fitted across the full diameter of the disc, use only the left half where the disc moves downward, thus holding the work down. Provided that the support platform is at 90° to the disc, rigid sanders can be used for producing true right angles in woodwork. Light pressure gives the most accurate results and the finest finish.

Always check that the sander's table is at right angles to the disc before using.

Attaching abrasive paper. While backing disc is rotating, spread on the adhesive.

Switch off, then press the abrasive disc on to the backing disc.

Only use the left half of the platform, where the disc is moving downward.

Abrasives, polishers and grinders

Use a wire brush [1] for the first stage in polishing corroded or slightly pitted metal. Follow up with the rag buff [2]. 'Dress' the rag buff before using, by applying a stick of polishing compound to the buff while it is rotating.

For final polishing, use the lambswool bonnet [3]. De-rusting of drain-pipes or other metalwork before repainting can be done with a wire cup brush [4].

Straight or tapered abrasive bands which fit over companion holders [5 and 6] can be used for sanding small objects or those which cannot be reached with the normal abrasive disc [7] attached to a flexible backing pad [8].

The power grinder [9] which is used in conjunction with grinding wheels [10] is designed for grinding and sharpening edge tools and knives. Adjustable supports on power grinders can be moved inward to compensate for grinding-wheel wear. For use, see p. 18.

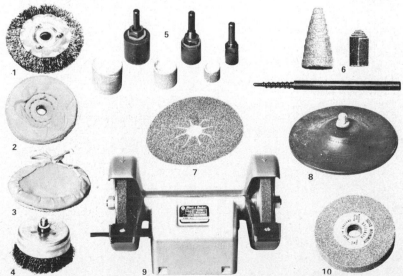

Finishing/5

Linseed oil

This is the cheapest of the oil finishes. It is available boiled or raw—the boiled form dries more quickly. Linseed oil takes longer than teak oil to apply but it has a greater depth of finish.

Drying can be speeded by adding a little Terebine (drier) and mixing it thoroughly with the oil. Terebine is obtainable from most ironmongers; do not confuse it with Terebene, which is used medicinally.

In common with other oil finishes, linseed oil is easy to use and needs no special preparation of the timber. Oils of all types darken the timber to give a tough, non-gloss finish without covering up the grain and texture. The finish is water-resistant and improves with age.

Resistance to damage is built up gradually over the years by additional applications of light coats of oil rubbed well in; resistance to heat and spirits is limited, but damage done by them to the finish is easily repaired.

Teak is the timber most suited to an oil finish. Afrormosia and iroka, often used as teak substitutes, also take oil well.

Rosewood, mahogany and oak can all be oiled, but light-coloured timbers, such as sycamore, ash and beech, become dirty and discoloured; softwoods, for ex-ample pine, are unsuitable for oil finishes.

Application: prepare a mixture of 1 part linseed oil and 1 part pure turpentine. Apply the mixture liberally, working it well into the timber across the grain with a brush or cloth.

Leave for an hour or two, then wipe off the surplus with a soft, dry, non-fluffy cloth. Leave for at least two days, then apply a second coat. Non-oily timbers may require up to four applications of the mixture.

Build up a sheen by hard rubbing with a soft cloth. Use a little wax polish to get a better finish.

Teak oil

This oil contains drying agents and varnishes which greatly speed up the drying process and give an improved resistance to marking, compared with pure linseed oil.

Use olive oil, which is odourless, in preference to teak oil or linseed oil, on articles which come into contact with food, such as salad bowls.
Application: apply liberally with a cloth or brush, working the oil well into the timber across the grain.

After about half an hour, wipe off the surplus oil and allow the surface to dry for at least eight hours before applying a second and much thinner coat. Do not aim to build up a coat on top of the timber; this can result only from too much oil being used.

When the second coat is dry—probably on the following day, or even later—rub down with fine steel wool (grade 00 or 000) impregnated with wax polish. Clean off with a dry, soft, non-fluffy cloth. Some non-oily timbers may require more than two coats of oil.

Destroy all cloths after use as they are self-igniting and highly inflammable.

Petroleum jelly

Vaseline can be used instead of oil for a finish but it is more difficult to apply. It is best used to give a finish to close-grained timbers, for instance teak and rosewood.
Application: rub the Vaseline well into the grain. Next day, rub off any surplus from the surface and buff up with a dry cloth. Vaseline fills the grain more than oil, but builds up a surface resistant to marking.

Wax polish

Traditionally, wax polishes were prepared from a mixture of beeswax, turpentine and carnauba wax. Modern wax polishes contain silicones and driers which cut down the work of application and give a better resistance to marking. Use a good silicone wax, not a cream or spray.

Wax polish can be applied direct to raw timber, but the finish will not be durable. It is more practical to seal the timber first with another finish, such as Ronseal, before applying the wax.

Wax finishes, like oil, have to be maintained and need more careful treatment than lacquer finishes. Their appearance, however, is pleasing, with a satin gloss that improves with age and can be quite easily repaired.

Most timbers can be successfully waxed. Oak, in particular, is well suited to waxing, but light-coloured timbers, such as sycamore and ash, tend to look dirty after a while as the wax works into the grain.

Use wax for maintaining or enhancing other finishes, such as oil or French polish.
Application: apply a light coat of the sealer by brush or cloth direct to the unfilled timber, working it well in and finishing evenly with the grain.

Allow to dry thoroughly, then sand lightly with fine abrasive paper. Some porous timbers may require two light coats, but do not apply any more than is needed to seal the surface.

Apply a heavy coat of wax by cloth or, on flat surfaces, with a stiff brush. Work it well into the timber and finish off by stroking with the grain before leaving to harden. Leave for several hours before rubbing up with a soft brush—a shoe brush is ideal. Finally, buff with the grain with a soft cloth.

For sealed timber, apply three coats (one heavy and two light) with a lapse of several days between each.

Polyurethane lacquer

This gives an extremely tough finish, superior to cellulose and French polish in its resistance to heat, water, spirits and abrasion. It is easy to apply and maintain.

One- and two-pack varieties are available. The two-pack varieties, containing separate lacquer and catalyst, are preferable where maximum toughness is required. In the one-pack varieties, such as Ronseal, lacquer and catalyst are pre-mixed and begin to cure on exposure to air. Do not use polyurethane lacquers on new floors.
Application: polyurethane lacquers are best applied direct to the sanded timber. If grain filling is required, use a special polyurethane filler.

For staining, use an acid-resistant pro-duct. If the manufacturers of the polyurethane do not specify a particular type, buy a water or naphtha stain.

With two-pack varieties, follow the maker's instructions carefully, as proportions of lacquer and catalyst to be mixed vary from make to make. Mix them thoroughly and allow the mixture to stand for five to ten minutes before use. Mix only enough for the job in hand, as the lacquer remains viable for only about 24 hours.

Apply the lacquer either by brush or by spray. Generally, a heavier film is less attractive in appearance but greater in resistance to damage than a lighter film.

For most jobs, such as shelves, bookcases and vertical surfaces, one or two coats should be sufficient. None of these lacquer finishes achieves maximum hardness in less than seven days, although they are touch-dry in four to six hours.

With brush application, lay the first coat across the grain and finish off by brushing out with the grain. Allow to dry overnight. Lightly sand with fine, dry abrasive paper before applying a second coat of polyurethane.

The final coat should also be sanded to remove high spots, then rubbed down (with the grain) with grade 00 or 000 steel wool. A thin coat of wax polish can then be applied if required.

If polishing unfilled timber, first remove any white deposit in the grain by wiping the surface with a cloth dampened with white spirit.

Transparent coloured polyurethane

Readily available are coloured polyurethane finishes which allow the natural grain of the wood to show. They give a tough surface which resists chipping, scratching and even boiling water.

They are excellent for use on new wood that has few blemishes and fillings. When choosing whitewood furniture to be finished with coloured polyurethane, select pieces with a good, unbroken grain.

Old wood that has been treated with paint, varnish or any other finish must be cleaned right down to the bare wood.

Application: clean off all grease and wax with an abrasive and white spirit; do not apply the finish in humid conditions.

Apply the first coat, preferably of clear Hardglaze, with a cloth pad. Leave this to dry for at least six hours, then apply further coats with a paint brush. If you wait for longer than 24 hours between coats, rub down the previous coat with fine glass-paper or a medium grade of steel wool.

Obtain a matt finish, if preferred to the normal glossy finish, by giving a final coat of clear Ronseal Mattcoat.

Clean treated surfaces with a damp cloth. In areas of heavy wear, apply a wax polish for added protection. Cloths used for application are highly inflammable, so destroy them after use.

Do not use these finishes on linoleum, thermoplastic, PVC or rubber.

Coloured polyurethane paint

One-pack opaque polyurethane paints are extremely tough and scratch-resistant and give an ideal finish for nursery and kitchen furniture. They withstand temperatures up to 100°C (212°F) without discolouring, and table tops in these finishes are not harmed by contact with hot plates.

Polyurethane paints are durable when used outdoors. They are available in gloss and eggshell finishes.

Application: no special preparation of the timber is necessary. After a coat of polyurethane primer, apply with a brush or spray unit in the same manner as ordinary paint.

For best results, lightly sand between coats, taking care to remove all dust and allowing not more than 24 hours between applications of successive coats.

Previously painted surfaces do not require priming but do need careful cleaning, to remove dirt and grease, followed by a light rubbing down with abrasive paper. Exposed surfaces need at least two coats; a single coat may suffice indoors if the new paint is much the same colour as the one it is covering.

Most polyurethane paints are touch-dry in about three hours, are ready for sanding within six to eight hours, and are fully hard after three or four days.

Clean brushes or spray equipment immediately after use with white spirit.

Floor sealers

Some floor sealers on the market, such as Bourne Seal, are also suitable for finishing general woodwork and some furniture. They are, in many ways, a compromise between oil and lacquer finishes and are well suited for wood finishing in the home.

They are applied in the same way as oil finishes. They penetrate deep into the timber and, like oil, tend to darken it. With successive coats, a fairly resistant film can be built up if required. This will not have the toughness of two-pack lacquers, but it can be repaired and recoated fairly easily; and with average wear and use it will require little maintenance.

Application: apply with a brush or a pad of non-fluffy cloth to the unfilled timber, working across the grain and well into it. Finish by brushing out or wiping off any surplus, this time working with the grain, before allowing to dry.

Drying is slow, and the surface is best left overnight. Lightly sand between coats to remove high spots.

On all vertical surfaces, such as panelling, and on shelving, one or two coats are sufficient. Leave the final coat for a few days before rubbing down, with the grain, with steel wool, grade 00 or 000. Remove dust and apply a thin coat of wax polish.

Horizontal surfaces, likely to have to withstand harder wear, may require three coats. Further coats can be applied periodically, but only after all traces of wax or grease have been removed.

These finishes can be applied to any timber and are well suited where the extreme hardness of two-pack lacquers is not essential.

French polish

This is a traditional finish and is applied to many valuable antiques. The basic material is shellac dissolved in methylated spirit.

There is little point in French polishing at home except on repair work and when matching existing furniture—although it provides an excellent finish, it is easily marked by heat and liquids.

Various proprietary brands of French polish make the job simpler for the amateur and, applied with care, give a satisfactory result.

Garnet polish, button polish, white polish and transparent polish are all forms of French polish, having a base of shellac and differing only in colour; true French polish is a rich brown, the others being degrees lighter, down to near-transparent.

Techniques in application vary according to the type of polish and the user's skill. The following serves as a general guide to polishing procedure and should be within the capabilities of a careful amateur.

Preparation: the timber must be well sanded and clean, and the grain filled with a grain filler. Choose the shade of polish you require, bearing in mind that darker polishes darken wood considerably. When matching colour, experiment first on sample pieces of timber. Any staining must be done before applying the polish.

Equipment: the most important implement in French polishing is the polishing rubber; it is with this simple tool that the best work is produced. It consists of a pad of cotton wool, which acts as a reservoir for the polish, and a cover of soft white linen or cotton fabric, similar to a well-worn handkerchief, which acts as a filter.

The rubber must never be dipped into the polish; it is charged by pouring the polish on to the pad with the cover removed. Avoid over-soaking the rubber; the polish should ooze slightly through the cover when a light pressure is applied.

Application: work evenly over the surface with a slow figure-of-eight motion until the timber is coated with a thin layer of polish. The object is to apply a series of thin coats, allowing only a few minutes for drying between coats. Make sure that corners and edges get their full share of polish.

When you have obtained a level and even-bodied surface, the work is ready for the second stage, spiriting off.

Allow the work to stand for at least eight hours, then take a fresh rubber with a double thickness of cover material and charge it with methylated spirit. Wring out until practically dry—the cover of the rubber should feel damp and no more. This is vital, as too much spirit will simply dissolve the polish.

The object of spiriting off is to remove the rubber marks and to give that brilliance of finish associated with French polish. The motion of the rubber should be the same as before, figure-of-eight, with increasing pressure as the rubber dries out. Replace the covers with fresh pieces of cloth from time to time.

Finally, work in the direction of the grain and continue until the surface is free from smears and rubber marks. Leave to harden off. French polish dries quickly but takes several days to acquire maximum hardness.

Shellac-based polishes can also be applied by brush, each coat being allowed to dry thoroughly and rubbed down lightly with fine abrasive paper.

The finish obtained in this way, whilst being satisfactory for many uses, does not compare with French polishing in quality of film and finish.

Other titles in this series:

THE USE AND CARE OF LAWN MOWERS 50p
HOME DECORATING 50p
LOOKING AFTER YOUR CAR 50p
THE MAINTENANCE OF BICYCLES AND MOPEDS 50p
HOME PLUMBING 50p
THE A–Z OF HOUSEHOLD REPAIRS *(in three parts)* 60p each
UNDERSTANDING PRACTICAL ELECTRICS 60p
MAKE YOUR OWN BREADS, CAKES AND PASTRY 70p
THE BEST OF MEAT *(available July 1976)* 70p

Where to buy Basic Guides

Basic Guides are available at W.H. Smith, John Menzies and all leading bookshops, newsagents and stationers.

They are also on sale at Reader's Digest Centres in London—in Berkeley Square, Essex Street and Old Bailey, and in Selfridges of Oxford Street and Barkers of Kensington High Street—and in the following stores outside London: Owen Owen of Bath, Rackhams of Birmingham, Beales of Bournemouth, Howells of Cardiff, Allders of Croydon, Schofields of Leeds, Rushworth and Dreaper of Liverpool, Dingles of Plymouth, Schofields of Sheffield and Binns of Sunderland.

In case of difficulty, write to Newsstand Circulation Department, Reader's Digest, 25 Berkeley Square, London W1X 6AB.

Published by The Reader's Digest Association Limited, 25 Berkeley Square, London W1X 6AB

First edition
Copyright © 1975 The Reader's Digest Association Limited
First reprint 1976

Printed in Great Britain by Varnicoat Limited, Pershore, Worcestershire